KLIMT

© 1989 Anaya Editoriale s.r.l./Fenice 2000 s.r.l., Milan
Created and produced by Fenice 2000 s.r.l., Milan, Italy
Text by Fernando Huici
Editorial direction by Lorenzo Camusso
Edited by Luca Selmi, Cecilia Lazzeri
Picture research by Francesca Bonfante
Translation by Sarah Hilditch
Separations by Sebi s.r.l., Milan
Typesetting by Fotocompograf s.r.l., Milan
Printed by Amilcare Pizzi S.p.A., Cinisello Balsamo (Milan)

This 1989 edition published by Arch Cape Press, a division of
dilithium Press, Ltd.
Distributed by Crown Publishers, Inc.
225 Park Avenue South, New York, New York 10003

Printed and bound in Italy

Library of Congress Cataloging in Publication Data
Klimt.
(The Masters gallery)
Bibliography: p.
1. Klimt, Gustav, 1862-1918-Catalogs. I. Title
II. Series.
ND511.5.K55A4 1989 759.36 89-178
ISBN 0-517-68374-1

hgfedc

FERNANDO HUICI

KLIMT

ARCH CAPE PRESS
NEW YORK

CONTENTS

Klimt and intellectual Vienna

In 1905 Gustav Klimt made one of his best and most interesting contributions to female portraiture, the genre that forms a central axis within his artistic production. This is the portrait of Margaret Stonborough, daughter of the great Austrian iron magnate Karl Wittgenstein, principal among the patrons who gave their backing to the Secessionists, that great movement of aesthetic renewal that marked the splendor of Austrian art between two centuries and that owned, in Klimt himself, one of its most paradigmatic members.

Two decades later, when the dream of the Secession of an art that would permeate the whole of the social fabric had passed away, mown down by the very process of dissolution that lacerated with profound contradictions the Hapsburg Empire, in the bosom of which that regenerative and aesthetic influence had been born, the portrait of Margaret Stonborough found an unusual frame in the house designed for the model by her brother, the philosopher Ludwig Wittgenstein.

Alessandra Comini has underlined the ironical paradox of this meeting between the work of the painter and that of the philosopher, between Klimt's delicate and sensual canvas and the ascetical and bare rigors of the building designed by Wittgenstein, the only work revealing his studies as an engineer, which was defined as "logic made building." Nevertheless, in spite of the evident visual contrast, this relationship is, in its more intimate significance, much less contradictory than it seems. Thus it is unfair and wrong to see it initially, as has certainly been done, as a mere Manichaean dissociation between a form of aesthetics that looks to the past and another opening toward the future: on the one hand one would have a sort of masking and uncritical decadence, an accommodating art that, even though unconsciously, would criticize and conceal a certain social order; and, on the other, ethical diligence with a strictly rational choice, in which art would cease to form a source of myths and dreams and become an instrument of knowledge and an analytical drawing of a new model of society.

Readings of this kind – today happily reviewed from a very different analytical perspective – have their origins in the progressive idealism that guided all the contemporary avant-garde traditions and that conditioned in a decisive manner the critical fortune of Klimt. Criticism has always felt itself obliged to recognize the central position occupied by this painter in the context of the Vienna of his age, but it has also often been disposed to relegate him to a marginal position in the more general panorama of this century, observing him as though he were a related episode and, in a certain anachronistic manner, a survivor of the 19th century who would never have been able to accept, with the exception of a few anecdotal appropriations, the challenge offered by the vanguard to his talent, which was otherwise undoubtable.

In spite of belonging to two quite distinct generations (Wittgenstein was 27 years younger than Klimt) their respective contributions as painter and philosopher – or architect, if we take our initial example – are, however, born from the same environment, that of the turbulent crossroads that was Vienna at the turn of the century.

We certainly cannot ignore the opposing attitudes that, starting from diverging theories, characterized the conflicts of that period. The famous proclamation of the architect Adolf Loos, which equates ornament and crime, together with its implicit criticism of Klimt's universe, constitutes an ideal example of this. Tracing the common questions to which these opposing options attempt to find an answer, or, even more, going back to the convictions that both one and the other share beneath their surface conflict, makes possible a greater and more profound understanding of the significance of their contributions to culture.

Thus, returning once again to our example, and following the analysis of Wittgenstein House made by Bernhard Leitner, we find ourselves faced with a vision of the project that is a long way from the idea of constructional rationality that presided over the debates of the architectural vanguard during the '20s; on the contrary, the essential theme of Wittgenstein's project is principally born, according to Leitner, from the symbolic function attributed to the spaces, the volumes, and the proportional relationships, a linguistic context, therefore, the essence of which was not foreign to Klimt.

The anecdote that unites the two personalities reflects the notion that it is possible to gather the true extent and significance of Klimt's contribution in light of the intimate and complex ties that his paintings and attitudes have less with certain coordinates of European art during his time than with certain key questions that crossed intellectual Vienna in that period, making it that which Cioran defined, with a reference to Karl Kraus, as a sort of "general thesis of the crisis in European cultural tradition."

In 1918, the year of Klimt's death, Wittgenstein completed the key work of his youth, the *Tractatus Logico-Philosophicus*, which placed him among the principal figures of contemporary thought. Despite the belittling reading that a certain branch of positivism has given it, what is certain is that this exemplary text, of crystalline simplicity, closes, rather than opens, through its reflection on the limits of language, one of the main questions that Viennese culture at the end of the century had posed itself. The works of Gustav Klimt, his concept of the destiny of the artist within society, and the postulations on the nature of reality – or on the impossibility of its knowledge – that run through his paintings are more precisely versions of an attempt to interrogate – or at least to show allegorically – starting from artistic intuition, that dramatic condition of the inexpressible that the *Tractatus* places beyond the limits of language.

Wittgenstein drew the fulcrum of his ideas from Schopenhauer – to whose works he had been introduced, it seems, by his sister Margaret – the philosopher who had a major impact on Viennese debate during the last decades of the 19th century.

Wittgenstein's interest was above all in the interpretation given by Schopenhauer to the Kantian epistemology, in his attempt to establish the internal limits of reason, leaving out the whole field of metaphysics. Starting from the Kantian concept according to which what we perceive is phenomenal – and therefore mere appearance – Schopenhauer himself identified reason and language, limiting the range of the latter to the description of our "representations." This problem – which limits the sphere of language according to the manner in which reality manifests itself to us, denying it any possibility of access to that which is its essence – had generated, in Austrian circles of thought, a vast debate around questions such as truth and the possibility of positive knowledge. Thanks to the study of the logic of propositions, carried out by Bertrand Russell and Gottlob Frege, the Wittgenstein of the *Tractatus* found a solution to this dilemma, starting from the equivalence of logical structure in language and reality. By establishing thus, in his turn, the borders of descriptive language, he was to cast the foundations on which it would be possible to construct scientific knowledge.

However, beyond this remained other aspects, such as ethics or the sense of the world, questions that could not sensibly be placed within language. It is to these that his celebrated final phrase – "Of that on which we are unable to speak, let us be silent" – refers.

The *Tractatus* thus considered as resolved this crucial problem of the European philosophical tradition, which had assumed a particular virulence in Austrian thinking circles. Without doubt, it is not easy to extrapolate into other fields aspects which are inherent to a philosophical discussion without making abuses. But, within this discussion on the positions maintained in the face of the problem of knowledge, the validity of metaphysics, or of the foundations of ethics, there is – even in Wittgenstein's own reply – a basis of skepticism that can be compared, in a network of more complex relationships, to the general spirit of the crisis that vertically crossed the whole of Viennese culture in the 1900s. We find, in this way, reflections of this crisis in the criticism of the empire as a model state, in which the illusion of unity and harmonic integration dissolves under the weight of multiple national identities and irreconcilable social tensions. But its significance is, fundamentally, that of the crumbling of all the concepts of subject and reality on which most of our culture was based. Thus, with Freud and his revolutionary studies on the subconscious and the part played by instinct, the dreams of humanitarianism and rationalist idealism vanish; with the psychologism of Ernst Mach's theories on the sensations, the gulf between the subject and the possibility of knowledge grow greater still. From Kraus to Musil and Broch himself, the perspectives that joined to form this critical conscience are innumerable. The very "bet" made by Wittgenstein himself on silence – as being the only coherent attitude in face of the limited condition of language – has a celebrated precedent in the anguish of the "unreality" that impregnated the fabric of Viennese culture; the reference is to the *Letter to Lord Chandlos*, by Hugo von Hofmannsthal, the protagonist of which rejects writing, crushed by the loss of significance of words.

Like the thoughts of Wittgenstein – although with the differences in detail proper to their differing generations – Klimt's painting buries its roots in the coordinates of this critical and turbulent Viennese landscape, and, in a particular way, in the impression that had been left in it by Schopenhauer. From this the eulogy with which Hermann Bahr hailed the painter, in 1903, as the ideal interpreter of an Austrian identity in which "everything dissolves into pure appearance." Following the line of influence started, in the decade beginning in 1879, by the Literary Association of German Students in Vienna, Bahr and Max Burckhardt had begun, in the quality of literary consultants for the paper *Ver Sacrum*, to actively spread the ideas of Schopenhauer, Nietzsche, and Wagner, determining in a decisive manner the dominant ideology within the Secession, both as regards a global concept of reality and as regards the place held by art within it.

Schopenhauer's line of thought attributed to art a transcendental role, that of an instrument which, by means of pure contemplation, permits a temporary liberation "from the slavery of freedom." Within this concept, which sees art as "a clear mirror of the world's being," a reflection of its essential identity, music has a very special role. The musician, according to Schopenhauer, can go even further than the metaphysician, transcending the limits of representation and, free from the ties of language, transmitting sentiments and convictions of a deeper type.

In some ways – although on a reduced plane – Wittgenstein himself presents a similar idea with reference to the function of art. This is demonstrated in the excellent study by Allan Janik and Stephen Toulmin on the Viennese environment that gave the *Tractatus* its origin. Egelman's idea – according to which the true objective of the book is exterior to the book itself, which Wittgenstein himself appears to confirm in a letter in which he states that "what is really important must be kept silent" – is that the author of the *Tractatus* was interested not so much in defending the possibility of objective knowledge as in the problem of the sphere of values and the sense of existence, which he defines as "that which is mystical." For the early Wittgenstein this is a route that is tragically forbidden to philosophy because philosophy is subject to language, but it can certainly be indirectly "shown" by means of artistic creation.

This is precisely the role assumed by Gustav Klimt when he stated, in his opening speech at the Kunstschau exhibition in 1908, that "only an ever more profound interpretation of life in all its forms, by way of artistic ideas, will permit the progress of culture." This concept of the artist as a privileged interpreter, beyond the knowledge of a phenomenon, of the inexpressible essence of reality, of his own being, impregnates the whole of Klimt's work and determines the sense of the singular evolution of his style. Thus, for example, his interest in mythological themes was to be tied to the Nietzschian idea of myth as an element provoking a Dionysian atonement that, by way of emotion, would permit a revelation capable of transcending the more immediate reality.

In some of his key works – and in particular in the celebrated *Beethoven Frieze* – Klimt also confers a paradigmatic value, within his idea of art, to music. And, in some ways, his continuous stylistic exploration can be considered a process of research into a sort of "musicalization" of the pictorial language, in which the progressive abstraction of signs and the emphasis on the sensual immediacy of ornament attempt to construct a choice of language that is capable of dissolving the allegorical background into an expression based on pure sensations, beyond codification.

However, in an even wider sense, the vision of the nature of reality that Klimt pursues in his works, by means of a pictorial formula capable of rendering it evident, is tied, in most of his themes and linguistic means, to many essential tracts of the same cosmogony proposed by Schopenhauer in *The World as Will and Idea*. In his synthesis of Kantian thought and that of the Oriental tradition, Schopenhauer saw, in space, in time, in the notion of cause, and in the division of subject and object, the four veils that keep us imprisoned in the world of representation, eclipsing any possibility of knowing their real being, which is will.

One must not fall into the trap of interpreting of Klimt's works as a literal and orthodox translation of the line of thought held by Schopenhauer. In the first place, the relationship is born not so much from a desire for a direct "philosophic" reading as from the general spread of these topics and their influence on the thinking public in Vienna at that time and, more particularly, on the ideological context of the Secessionist movement. Furthermore, even around similar concepts there are evident differences in attitude that define both personages. Thus, the pessimism that forms an essential part of the German philosopher's thought can be recognized only in certain periods of Klimt's career – for example, in the period of the panels for the Aula Magna of Vienna University – while in others he tends more toward what appears to be a form of idealism of hedonistic making. Then again, in his desire to articulate himself in a complex system of significance, the debt many aspects of Klimt's work owe Schopenhauer's formulations is clear.

In this way, the indeterminate ambiguity with which his painting breaks with the traditions of scenographic "reality" in the relationship between the figure and the background challenges both the identity of space and that of the subject itself, which is progressively reduced, in his work, to the mere illusion of certainty offered by the face, which becomes a focal point from which the figure dissolves into a chaos of ornament. In this preeminence of ornament, which for Bonito Oliva incarnates a reflection of the breakaway from every unifying concept of the world, characteristic of the Viennese fin-de-siècle, the plane of representation tends to convert itself into a pure surface, a plane bordered by a continuous and nonhierarchical illusory movement.

The impulse which, symbolically, is suggested as the hidden mover of this illusion of continuous generative vibration of the ornamental surface is in part indebted to the concept of "will" which Schopenhauer gives as an essential reality of the world, a power without either aim or object which, in some cases, can be compared with the body, opposed to the dual head-sphere of the representation. Klimt's painting represents the energy of this primordial mover, which hides itself behind the mirage of superficial reality and causes its multiform physiognomy, taking as a metaphor the binominal sex-sensuality and incarnating it primarily in the image of a woman, the absolute protagonist of his work, both in the portraits and the great allegorical themes.

Turning back to the dominant spirit of intellectual Vienna, the choice of Klimt approaches the concept of Karl Kraus, for whom man "has" sexual impulses, but woman "is" sexuality itself. And in Klimt's paintings, the plasticity and absolute maleability of the female nudes and the preeminence of epidermic sensuality that characterize his concept of ornament are in the end the same thing, figures of that energy without end or of that reason that substitutes the essence of reality and creates the dramatic illusion of that which is different.

In 1917, in a passionate speech, Peter Altemberg acclaimed Klimt as a philosopher and modern poet. He did not do so in a merely rhetorical spirit; like many other Austrian intellectuals of his time, he recognized in the artist's painting an eloquent expression of that discussion of the whole edifice of reality that constituted the most lucid contribution of Vienna to contemporary thought. Altemberg also underlined the fact that the "modernity" that Klimt reaches in his painting is superior, without doubt, to that attained by the "day-to-day" Klimt, the image of an abyss which opens before the unconscious intuition of the artist, capable, like Schopenhauer's musician, of "revealing the intimate essence of the world... in a language that even his own reason fails to comprehend."

In a manner that reveals his difference from the progress of the avant-garde, Gustav Klimt returns to the methods of his native environment, with its eclectic historicism, its symbolist tradition, its taste for stylization and ornament. But thanks to the uses he makes of them, these methods permit him to transcend their own surroundings, catapulting his art beyond the topics of the Secession until it achieves an incomparably complete expression of the central conflict of Viennese thought. It can be said that Klimt uses these methods to go "by them, beyond them," in a manner similar to that which Wittgenstein advises, in these same terms, to carry out the proposals of the *Tractatus*.

And at this point, without doubt, the meeting between the portrait and its surroundings that opened our discussion is now far from seeming a marriage "against nature." Both are born from a common environment. They are, perhaps, diverging mirrors, with differing natures and destinies – those of the thinker and those of the artist – but their reflections flow together fatally toward the shadows of the same uneasiness.

"Whoever wants to know about me... should study my pictures with care"

Max Eisler, in 1920, coined one of the most suggestive definitions of Gustav Klimt ever formulated by critical literature. "Time," he said, "is the destiny of his art." Naturally, by this Eisler was referring to the determinative influence, on the personality and works of Klimt, of the context of his age and, in a more specific sense, of the turbulent cultural and ideological scene in Vienna between the two centuries.

Klimt is the incarnation, more than any other artist, of the coordinates of that place and time. It is from them that his work is born, and to them he gives his most complete and profound reply. That age is Klimt's destiny, and it is so in an even more complex sense than that imagined by Eisler. Klimt's work, his concept of art, and his paintings themselves join all the essential aspects of his environment. This is also true for the nature of the conflicts which were generated in the Viennese world by Klimt's outlook: the more radical form of break, proposed in the following generation by Schiele and Kokoschka, which was closer to the direction of the European avant-garde and therefore worthy of greater fortune among the critics, was already outside the harmonic dream, then in its final phase, of the Hapsburg empire. Klimt's character as a disturber – for he disappointed the hopes placed in him as the interpreter of the dream that he ambiguously shared – was much more painful.

In his "solar" and "nocturnal" formulations, in his triumph as interpreter of the spirit of a society and an age, and in the amount of disturbance that the contradictions brought to light by his interpretation opened to the sight of official Vienna, Klimt is without equal.

The pillars on which the edifice of Gustav Klimt's work rises are essentially two. The first of these forms a part of the great symbolist tradition of the end of the last century, that is to say of the concept of painting as the vehicle, using allegorical expedients, for an argument regarding a certain philosophical or spiritual concept of the nature of realism. The second pillar is born from the preeminence given to everything that is ornamental within the complex of expressive values in his paintings. This corresponds to a concept of ornament, intended as a guarantee of the unity of style, which was common to all those modernist currents active at the end of the last century that defended the integration of the arts, and the abolition of hierarchical distinctions between art and craftsmanship, as instruments with which to arrive at a global, and idealized, picture of the environment.

What makes one understand the real greatness of Klimt, however – what gives him his place in history, indisputable although hard to define – are not so much these two choices, which all in all are present in most of Europe during that period, as the complexity of the system that he elaborated from them. Not only because his vision of the function of art and of the symbolic contents of his work, which are close to many of the questions dominant in the debates of Viennese thought at the end of the century, separate him from the slightly ingenuous mysticism of many other symbolist groups, but also, and above all, because Klimt developed, through the successive stages in the evolution of his language, an extremely sophisticated network of allegorical relationships that impregnate the ornamental signs and the pictorial relationships themselves with a significance that can be fundamental.

Far from breaking away from its roots, Klimt's attitude was born rather from an adventure to deepen and examine its roots. It is, in a certain sense, this trait of being limited to his roots that renders him liable to perish, according to a certain reading of history. However, at the same time, the same crisis in optimism of the avant-garde that characterizes the end of our century has, in recent years, caused a renewal of interest in that Vienna of 1900, in which a sort of prefiguration of many of the paradoxes that today grip the European conscience was seen. Under this light, the figure of Klimt assumes for us today an eloquent significance.

Through the retrospective view that time permits us, both the origins and the formative process of Gustav Klimt acquire the aspects of a premonition with respect to the cornerstones of his mature work. And, without doubt, we find in these precedents, in the precocious and systematic affinity for certain concepts that later occupy an essential place both within the works of the artist and in the debate that fed the Secessionist movement, some of the reasons for the natural affinity the painter felt for them, the profound knowledge he showed of them, and his possibility of approaching them in a dimension of ambitious complexity.

The first of these problems takes us back to the theme of craftsmanship and its relation to ornamental rules and techniques. The artist's father, Ernst Klimt, was a well-known goldsmith, and his influence directed three of his seven children toward specialization as craftsmen. Gustav himself, in 1876, entered – as did his brothers Ernst and Georg one year later – the School of Arts and Crafts of the Austrian Museum of Art and Industry. This school based its teaching methods on those of the South Kensington School of London, the teaching of which combined and equated the principal arts and the practical forms of crafts, an aspect of the Klimts' family life. It was in a borderland between the two options that Gustav and Ernst, who had chosen to orientate themselves toward painting, started on their creative road together. The group formed by the Klimt brothers and one of their fellow students, Franz Matsch, started a profitable career, in the decade from 1880, in the field of internal mural decorations, according to the style of the times. These years were still marked by the triumph of the Vienna of Ringstrasse, the wide encircling avenue that had taken the place of the ancient walls of the city and whose ambitious eclectic synthesis came to represent the self-satisfied character of the empire. In the sum total of all the various styles, the imperial society saw itself as the culmination and synthesis of history, tied to the past and at the same time a repository for all its successes.

The work of the Klimt-Matsch trio assimilated itself to the model of this eclectic synthesis and, in particular, to the example represented by Hans Makart, the best known and most popular Viennese painter of the second half of the 19th century. A creator of brilliant style and undoubted interest, Makart had become famous through his creation of large allegorical compositions in what must be considered a neo-rococo style.

There is, in the Klimt of this period, in this "Klimt before Klimt," one aspect of particular interest. His eclectic formation does not translate itself into merely an erudite assimilation of differing codes of style. Apart from this factor, which will in the end be crucial, the equivalent values that the various periods assume in historicism generated in Klimt his extremely characteristic type of knowledge of the relativity of language, which, as will be seen, becomes indispensable to the comprehension of certain aspects of his more mature works and, in particular, to the comprehension of the disinhibited spirit that marks his relationship with certain figures and movements in the European art of his time.

Without doubt, the influence of Makart, who made use of the collaboration of the Klimt group for some of his works, was a determinant factor during this period of the formation of the character of Gustav. Indeed, he would soon be hailed as Makart's successor. Although the imprint is shown in different ways (Werner Hofmann has pointed out, for example, the sensuality of Makart's female nudes as a precedent for the sensuality in Klimt's works) it has, at least in my opinion, a particular importance as an apprenticeship that involved styles and allegorical resources. Thus, in 1881, Klimt was given by the editor Martin Gerlach the job of illustrating "in Makart's manner" the work *Allegorien und Embleme*, a kind of systematical repertory that gathers together, at the same time, the history of artistic styles and the foundations of emblematic tradition. In fact, this idea of arrangement also characterizes the intent of the two principal works of Klimt and his group in the context of the Ringstrasse. His decorations for the Viennese Burgtheater retrace the fundamental stages of the history of theater, in the same way in which his paintings in the lunettes and between the columns of the stairway in the Kunsthistorisches Museum evoke the great artistic periods, from those of ancient Egypt and

Gustav Klimt in a photograph ca. 1908.

Rome to that of the Renaissance.

For all this, the works carried out in the second half of the eighties and at the start of the following decade show us a Klimt already a long way from the style of Makart, with an idealized realism of academic cut in the manner of Alma Tadema and certain heirs of the Pre-Raphaelite movement in English painting. Apart from the large mural works, Klimt's painting in those years unites two complementary paths that often merge. The principal of these keeps alive the symbolistic theme suggested, starting from the time of *Allegorien und Embleme*, by such edifying compositions as *Fable*. But virtuosity at realism also converts itself into chronicles and a celebration of the social environment that applaud the artist. A good example of this relationship is the spectacular view of the hall of the Burgtheater, in which Viennese society itself becomes the protagonist of the performance, and which gained the young Klimt, in 1890, the Emperor's Award.

On the death of Makart, the imperial state found in Klimt its new interpreter, an artist with a talent capable of maintaining the make-believe image of an intact and model empire when in fact the empire was attempting to survive itself, torn by potent internal tensions. As recognition of his skill – and after the work carried out in those two temples of Viennese culture, the theater and the museum – came a new commission of even more decisive significance: the decoration of the Aula Magna of Vienna

University. In the end, only Gustav and Franz carried out the project, as Ernst died in 1892. Gustav Klimt worked on the execution of three panels destined for the allegorical representation of *Philosophy*, *Medicine*, and *Law*, three disciplines that are also pillars of society and guarantees of the "common good." It is on them that the health of the spirit, the health of the individual, and the health of the social body ideally rest. However, positivist optimism, which thought to recognize in this triumvirate the reason for existence of a culture or of a state, in the end came up against a vision, in the interpretation developed by Klimt, that was deeply disturbing.

It was not only official Vienna, that of the empire and the ancient, grand, upper middle classes, that paid tribute to Klimt with admiration. His undoubted talent and his desire for renewal of the traditional models of official art also attracted to him the younger generation of Austrian artists, engaged in breaking away from the old forms and in searching for an art that did not delight in an ideal recreation of the past, but chose a new language suited to the "modern spirit." This, and no other, was the purpose finally engraved on the portico of the building designed by Josef Olbrich as the seat of the Secessionist movement: "To the age its art, to art its freedom."

Founded in 1897, on the model of the young German secessionists, the Viennese Secession, or "Union of Austrian Figurative Artists," was born from an intense yearning for reform. As proclaimed in the title of the paper which served as the organ for the spread of their ideals, *Ver Sacrum*, the Secessionist artists were searching for a "sacred spring," a new flowering that would permit them to break with the ancestral isolation and inconsequence of Austrian art. The promise of the Secessionists had its focal point, in the words of the architect Otto Wagner, in "the desire to show modern man his true face." On the one hand, this certainly involved the desire to unmask the concealing myths favored by academic historicism – history idealized as a refuge from the present – but, for the most part, the route proposed by Secessionism for the new art did no more than, as stated by Carl E. Schorske, "offer to modern man a refuge from the pressures of modern life." This was, decidedly, an essential contradiction of the Secessionist proposals: to oppose the poor spiritual idealism of the Ringstrasse with an aestheticizing environment which, again, represented a no less idealized rampart from which to defend oneself from the violent tensions in the crisis of Austrian society and culture.

In spite of this, apart from the restrictive and once again masking character of this "desire for style," the reflection and desire for renovation provoked by the Secessionist circle moved into much deeper waters and, in this sense, allowed the more or less conscious surfacing of several crucial questions. Due to its reformist, rather than truly revolutionary, character, the Secession should have been able to count on official backing, thanks to the politics embarked on by the minister Ernst von Koerber, who was searching for a safety valve to confront social tensions by resorting to the modernization of the economical and cultural spheres; however, as can be seen in Klimt's panels

Emilie Flöge, Klimt's companion for many years, in a 1901 portrait.

for the Aula Magna of the university, this aim of involving the Secession in works for the reorganization of the Imperial State – an aim that in many aspects coincided with the purpose of the Secessionists themselves – found itself frustrated by the nature of an allegorical form of address, whose vision of the world was hard for the state to assume.

The ideology that acted as a driving force for the Secession, as can be seen in writings such as those of Hermann Bahr, originated from that line of force, a key point in Viennese thought at the end of the last century, born from the dominant influence of Schopenhauer and Nietzsche. In the face of the liberal positivism incarnated by the Vienna of the Ringstrasse, which Loos – from the pages of *Ver Sacrum* before opposing his celebrated *Ornament and Crime* to the spirit of the Secession – described in a denigratory manner as a "Potemkin City," comparing Vienna to the cardboard decorations with which Potemkin, the minister of Catherine of Russia, simulated, during the passing of the royal carriage, the existence of prosperous villages where there were in actual fact only deserted regions, the Secessionist movement was to put into discussion both a progressive vision of history and science and the very validity of realism, contrasting a conception of art in which art assumes a transcendental role as an instrument of knowledge, in which, in the words of William McGrath, symbol and myth constitute the means to transcend and transform reality.

In the field of concrete plastic options, the Secession was in the end characterized by the development of a style marked by well-defined ornamental rules within the family of "art nouveau," but parallel to this it was to develop, pushed by its thirst for renovation and cosmopolitanism, a curiosity and a defence against all the other new European aesthetic currents of the moment, from symbolism to impressionism and their successors, in line with that eclectic aspect that was shared by all the modernist movements that – as was particularly clear in the case of Vienna – were born in a traditionally isolated context with respect to the larger currents for the renewal of European plastic arts during the second half of the nineteenth century. This two-fold desire, that of delimiting one's own style and that of permeability toward greatly differing styles of the new art (always from a certain type of dominant choice), confers a most singular identity to the contribution of the Secessionists.

No one better than Gustav Klimt – honorary member of the Secession from the very start and always hailed as its principal painter – was to translate the different facets of that mosaic, in their ideological content and formal reflection, into the definition of the "Secessionist style" and into the variations and nuances of an eclectic synthesis. Klimt is thus the paradigm of the Secession in its most topical vision, but he also penetrates into that topicality until passing the very boundaries of the movement. As far as eclectic appropriation is concerned, Klimt is a paradoxical case. The continuous variety of his works, the successive periods which mark drastic processes of redefinition, the on new models, the essential lines of restlessness in his subjects often start, both in the essential element and in the anecdote, with shameless appropriations from greatly varying artists or tendencies. This characteristic, which could be defined "Klimt-sponge," was to include along the way numerous examples, from Ferdinand Khnopff, to Stuck, Toorop, Hodler, or Rodin, right up to the formulas of impressionism, of Lautrec, or of van Gogh. The mechanism, in varying degrees, is always the same; he imitates aspects that interest him, but these aspects immediately assume a different, and very personal, weight within his language. It is of little importance that, in certain cases, they are taken from a lesser artist, because they are able to gain, during this process of assimilation, unexpected dimensions. At the same time, themes such as that of impressionism were used with an intent very different from that peculiar to them, being subjected to the symbolic ends typical of Klimt's painting. In a certain manner, this voracious passage of "modernity," which scans the evolution of its language, is nothing more, in its most immediate dimension, than an elongation of that

The house in Vienna where Klimt was born.

consciousness of the relativity of styles whose origins go back to the years of his eclectic formation.

Now firmly inserted in a process of reconstruction, Gustav Klimt began to take, under the influence of the initial debates of the Secession, a decisive turn toward that which can be considered the first real period of personal maturity in his work. Klimt ceases at this point to be a brilliant imitator and becomes the most singular personality in the new Austrian art. Among the works that best define this passage, which can be considered to have taken place in 1898-99, we will underline in particular two that, intimately related in theme and form, are in some ways the most precocious and decisive declarations of all that was represented by the Secession.

Pallas Athene, painted in 1898, constitutes one of the first examples of the use of the square shape that became one of the most characteristic constants throughout the career of Klimt and has a mythological theme that, as has already been indicated, has a programmatic value in all the central European secessionist movements. However, in the form proposed by Klimt, this allegory of the function of art as a desire for knowledge introduces a peculiar accent both in its iconography and in the expressive style used by the great Austrian painter. In the very image of the goddess we find ourselves already a long way from the chaste academic nudes of Klimt's first symbolist stage, the period of *Fable* and *Idylle*, but a long way also from the cold solemnity of the *Pallas* by Franz von Stuck, which Klimt took as his immediate model. But it is above all in the statue of Nike that the goddess holds in her hand that this difference becomes most palpable; in place of the bronze statuette painted by Stuck, Klimt presents us with a small nude of tangible sensuality, a "Victory" in flesh and blood that, as Alessandra Comini suggests, seems to introduce a completely different patron god: Eros.

One year later, Klimt gave this female nude with flaming hair the role of full protagonist in his *Nuda Veritas*, the naked truth, stripped of all veils. The "Socratic" mirror which this figure holds up to the spectator, inviting him to open himself to introspective conscience, has in a certain way a double theme; by putting us face to face with the reflection of our interior nature, that which can be seen in this new expression is the sphere of the

Klimt's studio on Feldmühlgasse, Vienna.

instincts, a long way from the ideal of the rationality of positivism. Carl E. Schorske insists on the "recognition" of this sensuality which colors, from this moment on, all the works of Klimt and which brings us back to a position that dominated Viennese thought at the end of the century, from the writings of Karl Kraus to the more obvious example of Sigmund Freud. In its initial formulation – which already extends, in the short period between the *Pallas* and *Nuda Veritas*, with other works such as *Moving Water* and *Nixies (Silver Fish)* – Klimt gathers together, in spirit and in form, the most common topics in the currents of eroticism, which run from a certain romantic tradition up to modernism. In a manner very different from the explicit laceration that sensuality presents in the works of the following generation of Viennese expressionists, the eroticism of Klimt, in its themes and in its expression, remains, throughout its extremely elaborate evolution, within basic parameters of allegorical idealization and formal stylization. However, apart from that which is usual in the context of eroticism at the turn of the century, the vision of woman and sensuality that forms one of the principal thematic cores of Klimt's work is not so much a literal reference as it is a pretext that translates a more transcendent reflection of character with respect to the nature of reality.

There is also another aspect to *Nuda Veritas* that must be underlined, that of the phrase from Schiller above the figure: "If you cannot delight everyone with your acts and your art, try at least to delight the few. It is not good to please the majority." The idea that art is necessarily destined for an elite – although a contradiction to the aim of integral representation of the environment and to the art "which makes no distinction between rich and poor, an art which benefits all," proclaimed by Hermann Bahr from the pages of *Ver Sacrum* – was to color the whole panorama of the Viennese Secession, and in Klimt assumes particularly fatalistic tones. The same idea can be found again on the occasion of his retrospective of 1903, under the evangelical form of "My kingdom is not of this world." In fact, both at the time of *Nuda Veritas* and in that of its later derivations, there throbs not only the background of the elite of the Secession itself – that is to say that of a community that opposes itself to the tradition of conven-

tions in taste and opens the doors to a new art conforming to the necessities of "modern" man, and consequently appreciated only by those minds alive to the true spirit of their time – but also the bitter personal experience of Klimt himself, in his efforts to reconcile faith in his character as an innovator with the type of conscience that moves with the powerful base of the official art that had given him his first successes.

The solidification of this break was to take place with the previously mentioned project for the decoration of the Aula Magna of Vienna University. As early as 1898 the initial sketches made by Klimt for his three panels had been criticized, but it was above all with the presentation of *Philosophy* in 1900 and of *Medicine* in 1901 that the scandal exploded to the point of shaking the whole context of Austrian cultural politics; the first of these paintings provoked a letter of protest signed by seventy-eight professors and divided the academic world into two factions; the reaction in the face of *Medicine*, which unleashed violent reactions in the conservative clubs, causing a scandal, seriously damaged the reformist project of Wilhelm von Hartel's cultural politics. As a consequence, although he maintained his backing of Klimt during the period of the crisis itself, the minister of culture later refused to ratify his nomination for a professorship in the Academy of Fine Arts.

The storm raised by Klimt's panels in the academic and political worlds of Vienna can be understood in the light of the abyss that separated the vision proposed by the artist from the hopes on which the commission had been based and which corresponded to the positive and rational tradition of the illuminist ideals. With respect to this concept, Klimt's allegories laid open to discussion the idea of progress tied to disciplines such as philosophy and medicine, offering a much more problematic reading of both. Using an expedient that is extremely frequent in his paintings, Klimt sets against one another two distinct planes of reality. In the *Philosophy*, within a notably "Schopenhauerian" conception, Klimt proposes an image of the world formed by an amalgamation of obscure forces which rises from the lower edge of the painting, with an illuminated face, representing knowledge, that is not so much an element of order imposing itself upon the chaos as a form of conscienceness of the unchangeably conflicting nature of reality. In a similar way, in *Medicine*, he paints a group of fluctuating bodies, representing suffering humanity, condemned to frailty and death, while in the foreground, Hygeia, who represents medicine, is incarnated in a female figure of implacable coldness, impassive in the face of a destiny which she is unable to halt.

To the tragic concept of these first two allegories, regarding which Hofmann rightly notes a debt to the idea of knowledge that Nietzsche opposes to the notion of science, can be added an even harder formulation with the final version of *Jurisprudence*, which abandons any attempt at conciliation with the academic world. Completed in 1907 under the influence, as noted by Peter Vergo, of the new expressive style first seen in that other great allegorical project, the *Beethoven Frieze*, the panel of

Jurisprudence shows us man as the victim of the labyrinths of legal administration, gripped by an enormous octopus. In the upper part of the work, isolated in an idealized plane, are the images of Truth, Justice, and Law; in the space around man is their real incarnation in the form of three Furies that persecute the impotent subject.

Destroyed, along with its two companions and other great works by Klimt, during the fire at Immendorf Castle in 1945, *Jurisprudence* symbolized the final breaking of the relationship between the artist and official Vienna, which had characterized the whole of the start of his career as a painter. At the same time, a link is formed with a new type of patron, which will condition all of his future work. When, faced with the impossibility of resolving his conflict with the university, Klimt decided to claim possession of the three panels, the iron magnate Karl Wittgenstein loaned him the necessary sum. Several years later, the panels were in their turn bought by August Lederer, principal among the collectors of Klimt's work and a figure of great importance in the railway and alcohol industries. Both these tycoons, who represent a sector of the Austrian upper middle classes, pioneers in the new fields of production, identified themselves with the innovative spirit of the Secession so much as to be converted to the role of major supporters. However, the change of patron was also to determine, in the case of Klimt, the type of commission, limiting the requests for large allegorical compositions in favor of other genres: landscapes and portraits.

Normally held in less esteem, within Klimt's production, with respect to other aspects of his work, the landscapes form a very interesting cycle. What is more, they reveal, on the basis of the primary position occupied by this genre in the initial context of the avant-garde, fundamental aspects of the type of relationship held by Klimt with some of the movements richest with novelty in the panorama of European painting. Thus, after the symbolist melancholy of his first landscapes, starting from 1900 we find ourselves confronted by the appropriation of motifs from impressionism and its successors, such as the works of van Gogh. One particularly interesting characteristic in many of these landscapes is the way in which the composition is forced until an undifferentiated surface is obtained, either by lowering the horizon or by raising it, in the manner of Monet's later works, to the opposite extreme, converting the horizontal representative plane almost into a vertical one. With this expedient, which can also be carried out by means of the complete preponderance of a vegetal surface, Klimt tends to identify – as he will also do in other points of his work, by then in the first years of the century – the plane surface being represented with the surface of the canvas itself. The evident "modernity" that this choice suggests must not, however, confuse us with regard to Klimt's intentions. In point of fact, his landscapes do not escape from the general symbolic trends of his other works, and nor do they presuppose, as in the dominant tradition of the historic avant-garde, a direct opposition to nature and a progressive abstraction of the pictorial language. On the contrary, Klimt develops

Franz Josef visits the first exhibition of the Viennese Secession (1898); drawing by Rudolf Bacher.

in his landscapes a sort of interiorization of the symbolic mechanisms, together with their removal. Stating, with regard to the landscapes, that "behind everything which Klimt created, the erotic remains," Richard Muther alludes precisely to the allegoric value of the sensuality that is dominant in his representation of nature, into which he translates the constant ferment of generating forces. In the same way his progressive identification with ornamental surfaces is a form of metaphor for the image of a world which for the subject can only be a front formed by mere sensations, without the possibility of acceding to its interior nature.

Although numerically speaking they can be compared to the landscapes (in both cases about fifty paintings have been catalogued), within the overall production of Klimt the portraits form a very unique case, which claims a much higher status and has had much greater fortune with critics. Even those detractors who, because of the determined rigidity of a certain puritanical view of the avant-garde, limit the larger significance of his symbolist proposal recognize as without discussion the innovative contribution made by him to contemporary portraiture. With the exception of a few initial examples of male portraiture, among which must be listed above all that of the pianist Joseph Pembauer and that of the actor Josef Lewinsky, Klimt dedicated himself almost exclusively to female portraits. The artist is said to have made the following statement in one of the rare written testimonies that have been left to us: "I am not interested in my own person as a 'pictorial object'; I am, rather, interested in other people, especially those of the female sex."

In around 1898-99 this genre reached initial maturity with the exquisite portraits of Sonja Knips and Serena Lederer, both influenced by the ethereal whites of Whistler. With these two portraits the double compositional model, on which Klimt was to concentrate right up to the variations of his final period, is seen to be established. The female figure, which is always posed in a position turned three quarters toward the spectator, appears seated on

Klimt in the garden of his Josefstädterstrasse studio; this photograph is from ca. 1910.

the right-hand side of the picture, when the painter uses the square form preferred by him, or standing, in an extremely stylized vertical form. However, the real great change can be seen in the portrait of Emilie Flöge, the woman to whom the painter remained sentimentally tied throughout his life. Underlining a tendency toward the dissolution of the figure's body into the background, which can already be noted in the case of the Lederer portrait, Klimt finds the formula that was to permit him to introduce into this instrumental genre an allegorical dimension that in the end rendered it one of the most significant bases of his whole aesthetic approach. It is once again ornament, in the ambiguousness of the figure's clothing and the decoration of the background, that allows the creation of a surface with indeterminate sensations in which only the presence of the face maintains the illusion of the subject. Thus, the individual woman takes on the role of a regenerating force, a role that Klimt awards her within his vision of the world. And progressively, as has been seen in the case of the landscapes, the most characteristic stages in the maturity of the painter were to accentuate this reference to the literal surface. With the portraits of Margaret Stonborough-Wittgenstein and Fritza Riedler, two culminating works that Klimt painted respectively in 1905 and 1906, we find a particularly interesting solution for the backgrounds. In spite of the clear architectural allusion in these works, the painter avoids any form of perspective, treating them as mere geometrical compositions on the surface of the canvas, in a concept that would have been a surprise because of the radical "modernity" of not knowing the symbolic value that the artist gives it. In the portrait of Riedler, Klimt also resorts to a new expedient, placing behind the woman's head one of the ornamental motifs which are repeated on the walls and that form a direct reference to the hair-style of Velázquez's *Maria of Austria* (painted in 1646), conserved in the Kunsthistorisches Museum.

But all the desire for symbolic meaning in Klimt's work does not exhaust itself in the landscapes and in the portraits, rendered more acute due to the crisis of the university paintings. On the contrary, the opening of the new century was to see the start of his principal allegoric period, including works that give definite expression to his aesthetic and metaphysical unrest. This series had a singular beginning in the exceptional drawing representing *January* in the calender of 1901, published by *Ver Sacrum*. The fact that the Secessionists conferred on Klimt the privilege of interpreting the image of the month that started a new century, without doubt finally destined to incarnate the realization of that "sacred spring" which they so ardently dreamed of, gives us an idea of the admiration they felt for an artist in whom they recognized their most stable guide. In the same manner, if we compare the emblematic complexity of the drawing of *January* with the illustrations of the other months, done by other Secessionist artists, the abyss of difference in which Klimt's talent stands out solitary from the overall context – limited though it is by the finitude of its time within the Viennese panorama – is clear.

Clearly derived from Nietzsche, Klimt's drawing places a number of figures in the space defined by a "uroboros," the serpent biting its tail in the archetypical representation of the circularity of time. To the left, a winged Cronus arises threatening, a figure which guarantees the fatal transience and passage of life. Standing on the back of the serpent of time, which returns incessantly, the naked figure of a young woman offers herself to father Cronus, in that crucial symbol which Klimt fixes in the female figure, sign of fertility and the inexhaustible potential of desire, which guarantees the eternal and undifferentiated mobility of nature. At the extreme opposite, also sitting on the "uroboros," an old woman wrapped in a dark mantle adopts the classical position of "melancholy," her chin resting on one hand, her gaze lost in the meditation of a destiny without reason or redemption. In this group of mythical references, which is magical in its pure simplicity and transparency, an enormous reflection of a philosophic order is without doubt opened.

The erotic theme, which is sustained by a two-fold argument, in the infinite maleability of the female nudes that fill, sometimes to the point of obsession, Klimt's sketchbooks, and by the explicit and immediate ornamental sensuality that caused the radical attacks of Adolf Loos, is thus converted into the central axis of Klimt's conversation, not as a literal obsession with desire, but as a mirror to a more profound vision of realism, that of a world divided between will and representation, which cannot be captured by the nets of language.

In certain allegories from the first decade of the century, and in particular in *Judith, I*, of 1901 and in that other surprising *Judith, II*, of 1909, which can today be seen at Venice's Galleria d'Arte Moderna, Klimt establishes a synthesis between the woman-creator and the woman bringer of death, conforming himself to the tragic tradition of the terrible romantic and symbolist heroines, beings that radiate a hypnotic and destructive magnetism, which Mario Praz has defined with unforgettably poetic precision as "medusan beauty." Moving away from this topic, which was without doubt widespread in the Vienna of that time, other works by Klimt elude the instinctive fear and the sense of blame which hide beneath this metaphor. Thus *Goldfish* insists on the energy "without attributes" given by the malleable and undulating bodies of the women, in a theme which is marked now in a more immodest form through the manifest obscenity of the lower figure, an attitude that will be repeated in the crudity of most of his mature drawings and in the introduction of lesbian themes, which are treated by Klimt with a naturalness foreign to morbid fascination, and in the drawings in which the sphere of desire remains totally without reference to masculinity. The autonomous character of this female desire, a guarantee of its metaphorical potential, continues to be ideally reflected in the abstraction and in the very corporeal circularity of the 1908 *Danae*. Another key work in this period, *Hope*, resolves the dichotomy between impulses of life and of death, which first appeared as integrated in *Judith*, returning to the opposition of two planes, that of the fertile potential of the pregnant woman's body and that of the threatening image of the finiteness and pain into which this potential will finally dissolve itself.

Apart from the thematic symbols, there is also, in the works of this period – and in particular in *Goldfish* – a compositional expedient of particular interest, which can also be found in certain of the landscapes. By this I refer to an organization of the composition in which the image goes beyond the borders of the painting and is cut off by them. Using this solution, forming without doubt an aspect of independent "modernity" which Klimt converts into a means for reaching the threshold of a greater symbolic complexity, the mutilation of the image breaks the very objective sacredness of the painting, which is thus converted into a mere instrumental window that allows a fragmentary view of a scene whose greater extension acts to multiply its "load of reality." At the same time, in an even more transcendental dimension, this idea of mutilation abounds in the limited character of all knowledge and in its incapability to conceive the world as a whole.

From the most ambitious projects of Klimt's career it seems possible to discern a sort of fatality. We have already seen what happened to the panels of the Aula Magna, first deprived of the setting for which they had been created and, later, destroyed by fire. Something similar to this was to happen to that other great allegoric cycle, the *Beethoven Frieze*, in which Klimt developed his fundamental arguments regarding the sense of artistic creation. Initially, an evident contradiction existed between the ambitiousness of the project, the masterly dimensions that its execution reached on completion – determining an essential turning in the language of its author – and the ephemeral character of its support and the function to which it was destined. Conceived so that it could be destroyed after having performed its role as a scenic background, it was in the end saved thanks to the zeal of the collector August Lederer (to whom, it must be remembered, the works destroyed in the Immendorf fire

Dining room of the Stoclet Palace, Brussels, decorated with mosaics by Klimt (1905-9).

also belonged); but due to the fragility of its support material – it is formed by seven large casein paintings on stuccoed canvas – serious conservation problems occurred, and it remained inaccessible to the public for many decades. Today, finally, after a long process of restoration and consolidation, the paintings are once more to be found in their original setting in the Palace of the Secession in Vienna.

The frieze had its origin in one of the most celebrated collective manifestations of the Secession, the exhibition of 1902 in which were presented, in the headquarters of the movement, the famous and spectacular *Monument to Beethoven*, by Max Klinger, within an ambitious scenographic surround designed by Josef Hoffmann. The exhibition – in particular because of Klimt's frieze – ended by becoming a transcendental homage to the composer, the latter incarnating the romantic paradigm of the artist-superman. The theme chosen by Klimt is based on a recreation of the final movement of the Ninth Symphony, which once again rests on the poetry of Schiller, through the verses of his "Hymn to Joy." On the occasion of the inauguration of the exhibition, Gustav Mahler directed a version of the work, in his own arrangement for stringed instruments.

Peter Vergo and Carl E. Schorske have pointed out the influence – yet again! – of the thoughts of Schopenhauer and Nietzsche on the conception of the frieze, an influence that was to be determined in this case by the interpretation which Wagner gave to Beethoven. In point of fact, the concept of music as the mediating entity par excellence, opening the awareness of the instinctive world, is a recurrent theme in Klimt's work. We find it already, during his first symbolist phase, in the subject of the twin panels to *Schubert at the Piano*, both belonging to the decorations of Dumba Palace, carried out in 1898. Equally, the very figure of *Music* in the *Beethoven Frieze* is literally inspired by a previous version (1895) of the same theme.

In a certain sense, the frieze has been interpreted as a

The headquarters of the Viennese Secession, designed by Josef Olbrich in 1898.

reply to the tragic questions posed by the three panels of the university. It is thus that Werner Hofmann expresses it: "It is not by way of philosophy 'Ex cathedra' that man will be able to reach the truth, it is not the progress of medicine which will free him from his torments, neither is it law, converted into a sumptuous façade, which will protect him from the voracious arbitrariness of the Furies. Only the work of art, in which the ability of the individual is manifested, will give the blind man back his sight, freeing him from his incessant search and his vain desire, transforming him into an aesthetic spectator." And, in effect, the *Beethoven Frieze* is intended as a voyage of initiation in which the artist, dressed in shining armor and with a visage eloquently inspired by the features of Mahler, has to confront a land infested by obscure powers, until reaching music, which will give him access to the kingdom of harmonic awareness, where he will be able to melt into an embrace that cancels all conflicts.

The *Beethoven Frieze*, however, is also the symbol of another kind of transformation, which gave rise to another change in the expressive language of Klimt, who, in fact, from this moment onward, moves away from the sinuous lines that are closer to southern modernism to create that geometry of artistic stylizations that was to end by imposing itself as the distinctive feature of the ornamental models of the "Secessionist style." At this point, Klimt was to have the opportunity of living a new paradigmatical encounter during his visit to Ravenna, when he became fascinated by the discovery of the Byzantine mosaics. The influence of this visit, which Wilhelm Dessauer defined as the "fulfilment of Klimt's destiny," flows into the celebrated golden period, which is often unjustly considered the culmination of a creative path which, as has been seen, comprises much more complex aspects. In any case, the "golden" stage corresponds to a relatively limited sector of Klimt's production; but its frontiers are often ambiguous, because of the interest for the ornamental possibilities of gold which the artist shows in various periods of his

evolution. The origin of this interest is without doubt to be found in the formation of Klimt in the context of applied arts. Within his pictorial works it was to assume an initial importance during the first symbolist period, limited, at that time, due to the pre-Raphaelite influence, to the decoration of the frame, and prevalently fruit of the collaboration as a goldsmith with his brother Ernst. In works such as *Pallas Athene* and *Nuda Veritas* we are witnessing a tradition that incorporated gold into the process of assimilation of ornamental techniques into painting itself, and with this significance it will be used in the *Beethoven Frieze* and in many other works. But it is certain that, at the end of the first decade of this century, the treatment of gold in Klimt's work assumes a different weight, within a process, the most eloquent examples of which are the portrait of Adele Bloch-Bauer and the well-known *Kiss* of 1907-8. This preeminence of gold coincides with that of an extremely complex system of geometrical symbols that practically devour the ground from under the other pictorial means, transporting the allegorical function once again until it rests not on narrative elements or systems of representation, but on a system of abstract signs.

The apex of this process brings us to the last of the great mural works carried out by Klimt, the decoration of the palace belonging to the banker Adolf Stoclet, in Brussels. Various paradoxical lines come together in this project. In the first place, there is the fact that – in an artist whose formation and ideological environment had turned on an idea of integration of the arts that would cancel every distinction between greater and lesser arts – this (and so late in his career) is the only case of real and equal collaboration with the productions of craftsmen. Klimt did no more than draw the sketches of the distinct motifs, which were realized in ceramics by the Wiener Werkstätte. But, on the other hand, and returning in part to the idea of that fatal destiny to which we alluded when speaking of the panels of the Aula Magna and the *Beethoven Frieze*, one cannot cease to be amazed that the only Klimt work that truly conforms to the Secessionist dream of an art "made by all," artists and craftsmen working side by side, and "for all," rich and poor, was in the end situated in an essentially private and well-to-do space, the banker Sto-clet's dining room.

On his death in 1918 – in the same year as that of the architect Otto Wagner and the painters Ferdinand Hodler and Egon Schiele, three figures to which the artist was closely linked – Gustav Klimt was fifty-six, an age that is still synonymous with full creative vitality. This final Klimt, however, was no longer the Klimt of the golden symbols. During the last six years of his life he had once again given a Copernican change to the direction of his language. After a few distractions marked by the influence of Toulouse-Lautrec, this new and spectacular final stage started, symbolically, with a second portrait of Adele Bloch-Bauer. Starting from this painting, not only does he break with the type which his portraits had essentially maintained up to that point, giving way to an absolute frontality in the position of the models, but he also adopts a radically new pictorial technique, in which the color is enriched with "fauve" accents and the brush strokes acquire a fluid sensuality. Finally, the new portrait of Adele Bloch-Bauer also introduces a new and suggestive expedient, which attains its best formulation in the superb portraits of the Baroness Elisabeth Bachofen-Echt and Friedericke Maria Beer, and which also tints that delicate late masterpiece which is *Friends*. I am referring, naturally, to the use of Far Eastern motifs in the decoration of the backgrounds, a theme that Klimt already knew well from the start of the century, but which does not appear in his work until this moment; the sixth Secessionist exhibition, which took place in January 1900, had been dedicated to Japanese art, and Klimt owned a collection of Korean paintings, which are often incorporated into the portraits of this period.

Even in the diversity of their execution, these last portraits continue to maintain interest because of the approach of the background plane up to the literal surface of the canvas, and for the melting of the edges of the figure into the ornamental surroundings, a process of spacial confusion that the Oriental scenes tend to increase. The pre-eminence of color and ornament, the reference to the real plane of the canvas, the fluidity, are factors that bring to mind Matisse, an association which such works as the portrait of Johann Staude or *Friends* do not render bold.

The dynamic force of the compositions and the looseness of execution also characterize the allegorical scenes of this final period. With the exception of one work, *Adam and Eve*, all the others seem to be variations on the same theme. In *Life and Death*, the first in order of time, a photographic testimonial of the initial version permits us to follow the steps that conduct us from the last elongations of geometrical symbolism into the new style. This metamorphosis, which opposes the phallic column of death to a rigid amalgamation of bodies, terminates in two masses of much more sensual identity, naturally akin to each other, and whose opposition is now lacking the dramatic radicality of other versions of this theme confronted by Klimt in the past. The flow of bodies, which appear to dematerialize into a constellation of areas of color, in which the painter reflects life, defines a model which is punctually repeated, although in a progressive liquid disintegration, in works such as *The Virgin*, *Baby*, and *The Bride*, which the death of the artist was to leave incomplete. The last two of these canvases, however, seem to indicate a departure from the aromatic sensuality of the late Klimt, to enter a more expressionistic phase, once again pushed by the incessant search that characterized the errant destiny of Klimt, who was by then beyond the limits of the time allotted to him but moving toward a horizon with luminous edges, similar to those of desire.

A drawing of Klimt's Nuda Veritas *appeared in* Ver Sacrum *in March 1898; he made the painting in 1899.*
The inscription above the figure reads: "Truth is a fire, and to speak the truth means to shine and burn."

Works

1. Allegory of Sculpture, *1889;*
Vienna, Österreichisches Museum für Angewandte Kunst; 43.5 x 30 cm

2.Sculpture, *1896; Vienna, Historisches Museum der Stadt Wien; 41.8 x 31.3 cm*

3. Tragödie (Tragedy), 1897; Vienna, Historisches Museum der Stadt Wien; 41.9 x 30.8 cm
This is one of the drawings made for Allegorien und Embleme, *published by the Vienna
publishing company Gerlach & Schenk.*

4.Young Girl with Lowered Head, *1898; Vienna, Historisches Museum der Stadt Wien; 45 x 31.6 cm*

5. *Junius, 1896; Vienna, Historisches Museum der Stadt Wien; 41.5 x 31 cm*
In this drawing, Klimt used for the first time the square format that he later used,
most of all for landscapes.

6. Portrait of a Girl, *1902; Vienna, Historisches Museum der Stadt Wien; 45.2 x 31.9 cm*

7. Crouching Female Figure, *1908-9; Vienna, Historisches Museum der Stadt Wien; 54.9 x 34.8 cm*

8. Fable, 1883; Vienna, Historisches Museum der Stadt Wien; 84.5 x 117 cm
This painting is derived from the illustrations Klimt made for Allegorien und Embleme,
edited by Martin Gerlach with text by Albert Ilg. For that publication Klimt
created designs with allegorical images.

9. Theater in Taormina, *1886-88; Vienna, Burgtheater; 750 x 400 cm*
Between 1886 and 1888, Klimt, his brother Ernst, and the painter Franz Matsch decorated the entryway
and stairways of the Burgtheater; this is a detail.

10. Music, I, 1895; Munich Bayerische
Staatsgemäldesammlungen, Neue Pinakothek; 37 x 44.5 cm
The lyre as motif and allegorical symbols of fin de
siècle culture, such as the sphinx and lion's teeth,
stand out in the composition of this work.

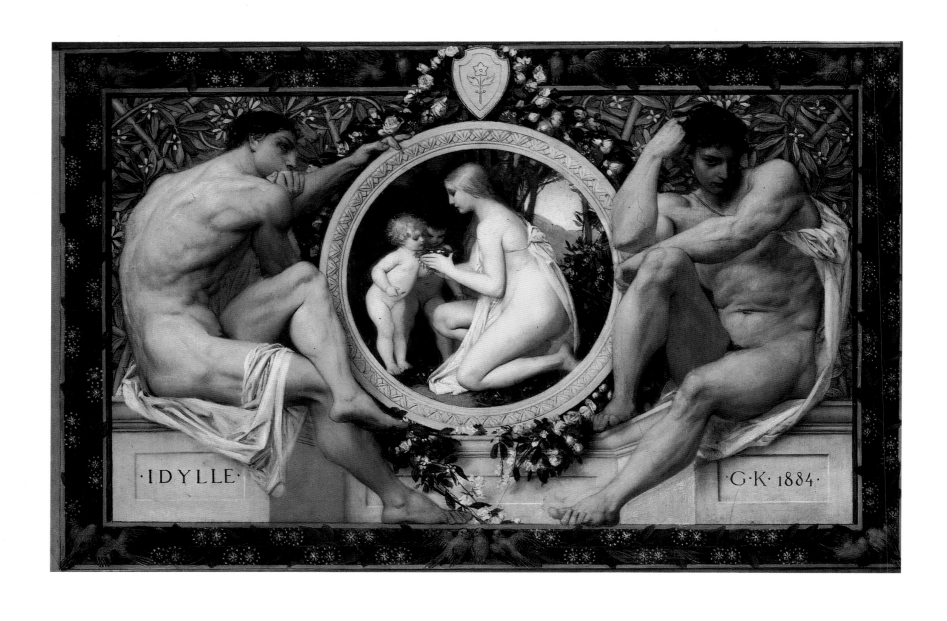

11. Idylle (Idylls), *1884; Vienna, Historisches Museum der Stadt Wien; 49.5 x 73.5 cm*
The composition and the figures of the nude males show inspiration from
the works of Michelangelo and Annibale Carracci.

12. Auditorium of the Altes Burgtheater, Vienna, 1888; Vienna, Historisches Museum der Stadt Wien; 82 x 92 cm
This painting, which shows the old Burgtheater before its reconstruction, is considered
the best example of Klimt's "photographic realism."

13. Sappho, 1888-90; Vienna, Historisches Museum der Stadt Wien; 39 x 31.6 cm
In this work, Klimt was inspired by the sensual and ambiguous atmosphere of the paintings of the French artist Gustave Moreau.

14. Portrait of Joseph Pembauer, 1890; Innsbruck, Tiroles Landesmuseum Ferdinandeum; 69 x 55 cm
The contrast between the "photographic" style of the portrait and the decoration of the frame, inspired by the Pre-Raphaelites, is clear.

15. Portrait of a Lady, *1894; Vienna, Historisches Museum der Stadt Wien; 30 x 23 cm*

16. Portrait of Sonja Knips, *1898; Vienna, Österreichische Galerie; 145 x 145 cm*
This painting, very well received by critics, has been shown in many international
exhibitions, including the second exhibition of the Viennese Secession in 1898 and
the 1958 Venice Biennale.

17. **Portrait of Josef Lewinsky,** *1895; Vienna, Österreichische Galerie; 64 x 44 cm*
In this portrait Klimt partly abandons photographic realism and presents a
psychological interpretation of the actor.

18. Love, 1895; Vienna, Historisches Museum der Stadt Wien; 60 x 44 cm
This painting, with its dreamlike atmosphere, signals the symbolist turn in Klimt's work.

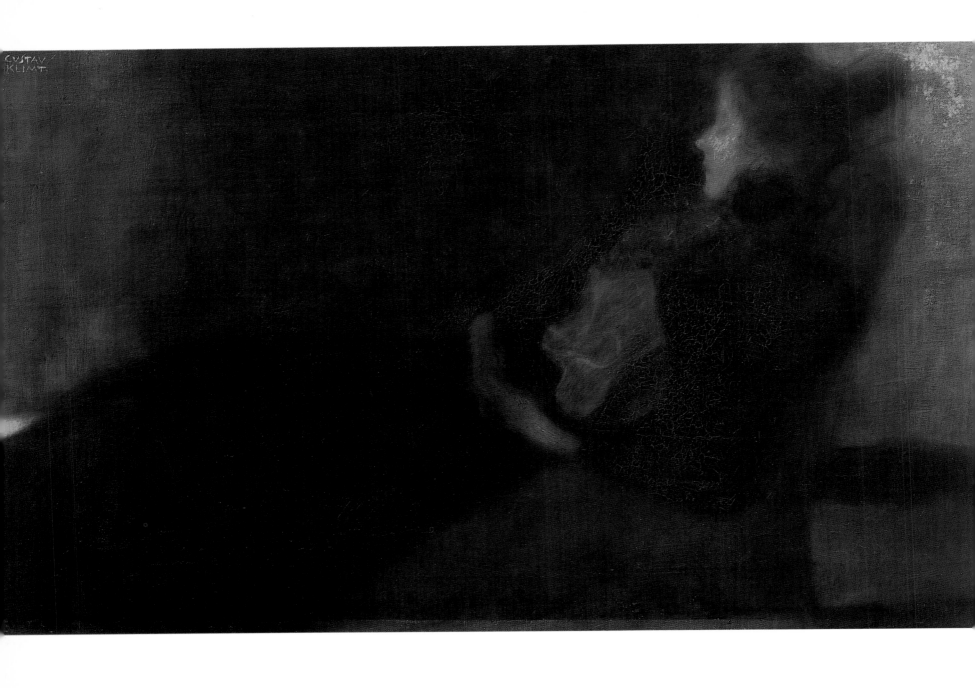

19. *Above:* Lady by the Fireplace, *1897-98; Vienna, Österreichische Galerie; 41 x 66 cm*
Within the asymmetrical composition of this work, the fusion of the chair, dress, and
background constitutes one of the formal elements in Klimt's portraits of women.
20. *Opposite:* Full-face Portrait of a Lady, *1898-99; Vienna, Österreichische Galerie; 45 x 34 cm* ▶
The lowered perspective presented in this portrait creates a pyramid effect
that can be found in other works by Klimt.

21. Pallas Athene, *1898; Vienna, Historisches Museum der Stadt Wien; 75 x 75 cm*
The figure of the Greek goddess was a recurring symbol in the Austrian-German area.

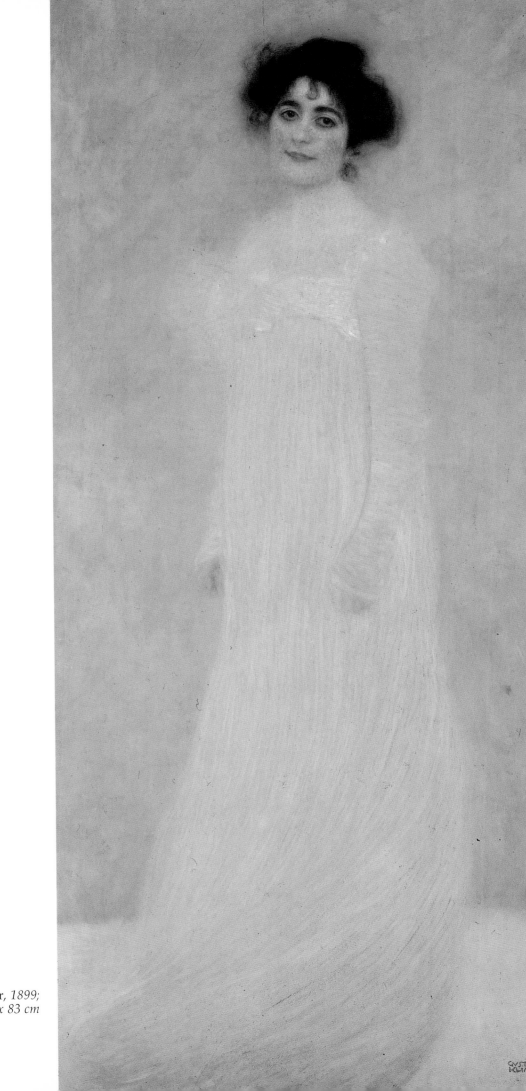

22. Portrait of Serena Lederer, *1899;*
New York, Metropolitan Museum of Art; 188 x 83 cm

23. Judith, I, *1901; Österreichische Galerie; 84 x 42 cm*
This painting is inside a frame of hammered
copper that was probably made by Georg Klimt
based on a design by Gustav.

*24. Portrait of Emilie Flöge, 1902; Vienna,
Historisches Museum der Stadt Wien; 178 x 80 cm
Emilie Flöge owned a fashionable dressmaking
shop for which Klimt made designs of clothing.*

25. Cows in a Stall, 1900-1; Linz, Neue Galerie der Stadt Linz, Wolfgang-Gurlitt-Museum; 75 x 76.5 cm
Only rarely did Klimt use animals as subjects for paintings.

26. After the Rain (Garden with Chickens in
St. Agatha), *1899; Linz, Neue Galerie der Stadt
Linz, Wolfgang-Gurlitt-Museum (in deposit at the
Österreichische Galerie in Vienna); 80.3 x 40 cm*

27. Farmhouse with Birch Trees, *1900; Vienna, Österreichische Galerie; 80 x 80 cm*
The horizon line appears high, and the trunks of the trees intensify
the created perspective.

28. Beech Forest, I, *ca. 1902; Dresden, Staatliche Kunstsammlungen, Gemäldegalerie Neue Meister; 100 x 100 cm*
The painting first appeared at the seventeenth exhibition of the Viennese Secession in 1903.

29. The Beethoven Frieze: The Hostile Powers (far wall), 1902; Vienna, Österreichische Galerie
This panel, and others reproduced on the following pages, was part of the decorations
Klimt made in 1902 for a hall at the fourteenth exhibition of the Secession at Vienna,
produced by Josef Hoffmann and dedicated to Beethoven.

30. The Beethoven Frieze: The Longing for Happiness *(left wall), 1902;*
Vienna, Österreichische Galerie
The geometric decoration of the second phase of Art Nouveau is here joined
to curvilinear elements taken from Japanese art.

31. The Beethoven Frieze: The Longing for Happiness Finds Repose in Poetry *(right wall), 1902;*
Vienna, Österreichische Galerie

32. The Beethoven Frieze: The Longing for Happiness Finds Repose in Poetry *(right wall)*, 1902;
Vienna; Österreichische Galerie

33. The Beethoven Frieze: The Longing for Happiness Finds Repose in Poetry *(right wall) 1902;*
Vienna, Österreichische Galerie
Klimt later used the theme of the embrace, a symbol of pure love, in The Kiss.

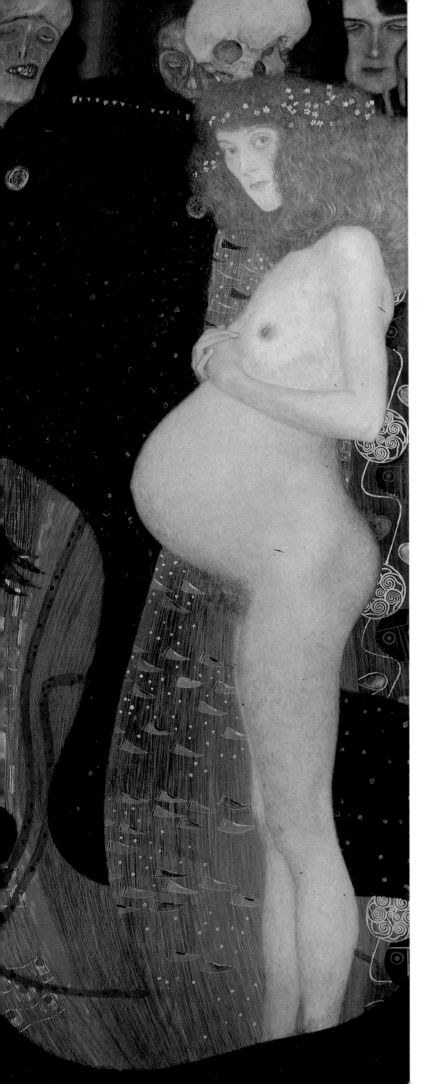

34. Hope, I, 1903; Ottawa, National Gallery of Canada; 181 x 67 cm
The composition is based on the juxtaposition of
the realism of the female nude and the indefiniteness of the aquatic figure.

35. Pear Tree, 1903; Cambridge (Mass.), Fogg Art Museum, Harvard University; 100 x 100 cm
In this work Klimt shows the influence of the pointillism of the Neo-Impressionists, to whom was
dedicated the sixteenth show of the Viennese Secession of January-February 1903.

36. Farmhouse with Birch Trees, *1903; Vienna, Österreichische Galerie; 110 x 110 cm*

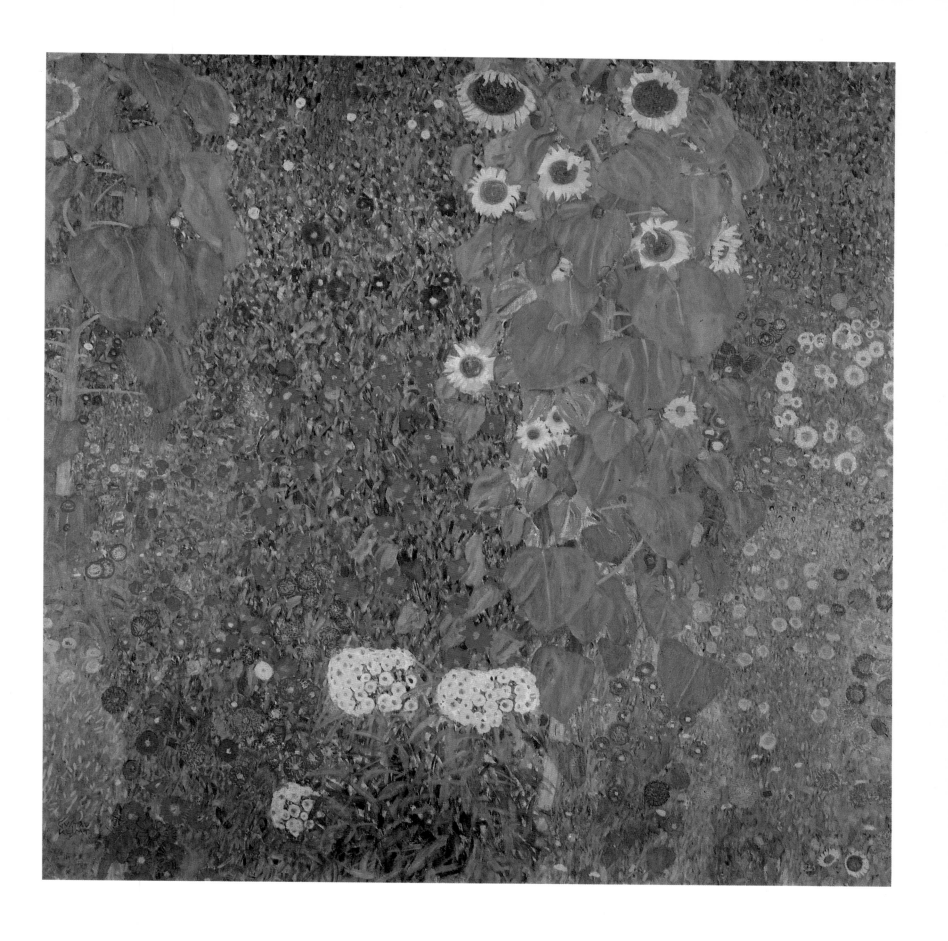

*37. Farm Garden with Sunflowers, ca. 1905-6; Vienna, Österreichische Galerie; 110 x 110 cm
Klimt painted this in the garden of an inn while vacationing at Litzberg on the Attersee.*

*38. Portrait of Hermine
Gallia, 1904; London, National
Gallery; 170.5 x 96.5 cm
This portrait presents
geometric elements,
particularly in the dress
and carpet.*

39. Portrait of Margaret Stonborough-
Wittgenstein, *1905; Munich, Bayerische
Staatsgemäldesammlungen, Neue
Pinakothek; 180 x 90 cm
This painting was shown at the Berlin
exhibition of the Deutscher
Künstlerbund in 1905.*

40. *Above:* Portrait of Adele Bloch-Bauer, 1907; Vienna, Österreichische Galerie; 138 x 138 cm
The abundance of decorative elements obscures the relationship between the figure
and the background; only the face emerges.
41. *Opposite:* Portrait of Fritza Riedler, 1906; Vienna, Österreichische Galerie; 153 x 133 cm ▶
This is the most important portrait of Klimt's geometric period; pseudoplastic elements taken from
the architecture of Josef Hoffmann are inserted on the surface of the background.

42. Above: Water Serpents, *1904-7; Vienna, Österreichische Galerie; 50 x 20 cm*
43. Opposite: The Three Ages of Woman, *1905; Rome, Galleria Nazionale d'Arte Moderna; 180 x 180 cm* ▶
Klimt won a gold medal at the International Exposition of Art at Rome in 1911 with this painting.

44. *Poppy Field, 1907; Vienna, Österreichische Galerie; 110 x 110 cm*
The trees, so very important in Klimt's early landscapes, are mixed in a composition
with a foreground full of brightly colored flowers.

45. Flowering Field, *ca. 1909; Pittsburgh, Museum of Art, Carnegie Institute; 100.5 x 100.5 cm*

◄ 46. *Opposite:* The Kiss, *1907-8; Vienna, Österreichische Galerie; 180 x 180 cm*
In this work Klimt makes use of themes with which he had experimented in earlier works,
such as the embrace, geometric decorative elements, and the flowering field.
47. Right: Judith, II, *1909; Venice, Galleria d'Arte Moderna; 178 x 46 cm*
This work, also known as Salome, *develops themes Klimt had used in 1901; in 1909 it*
was shown at the exhibition of the Kunstschau Wien, of which Klimt was president.

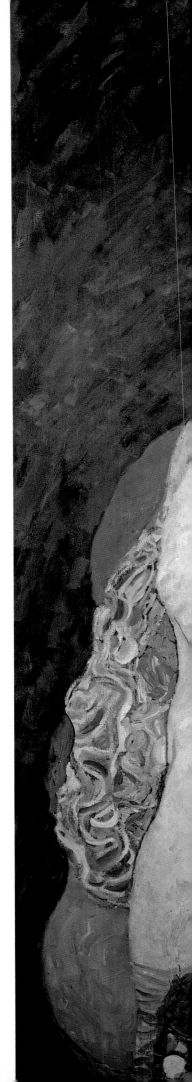

48. The Virgin, 1912-13; Prague, Národni Galerie; 190 x 200 cm
Compared to preceding works, this composition shows the signs of a more driven dynamism.

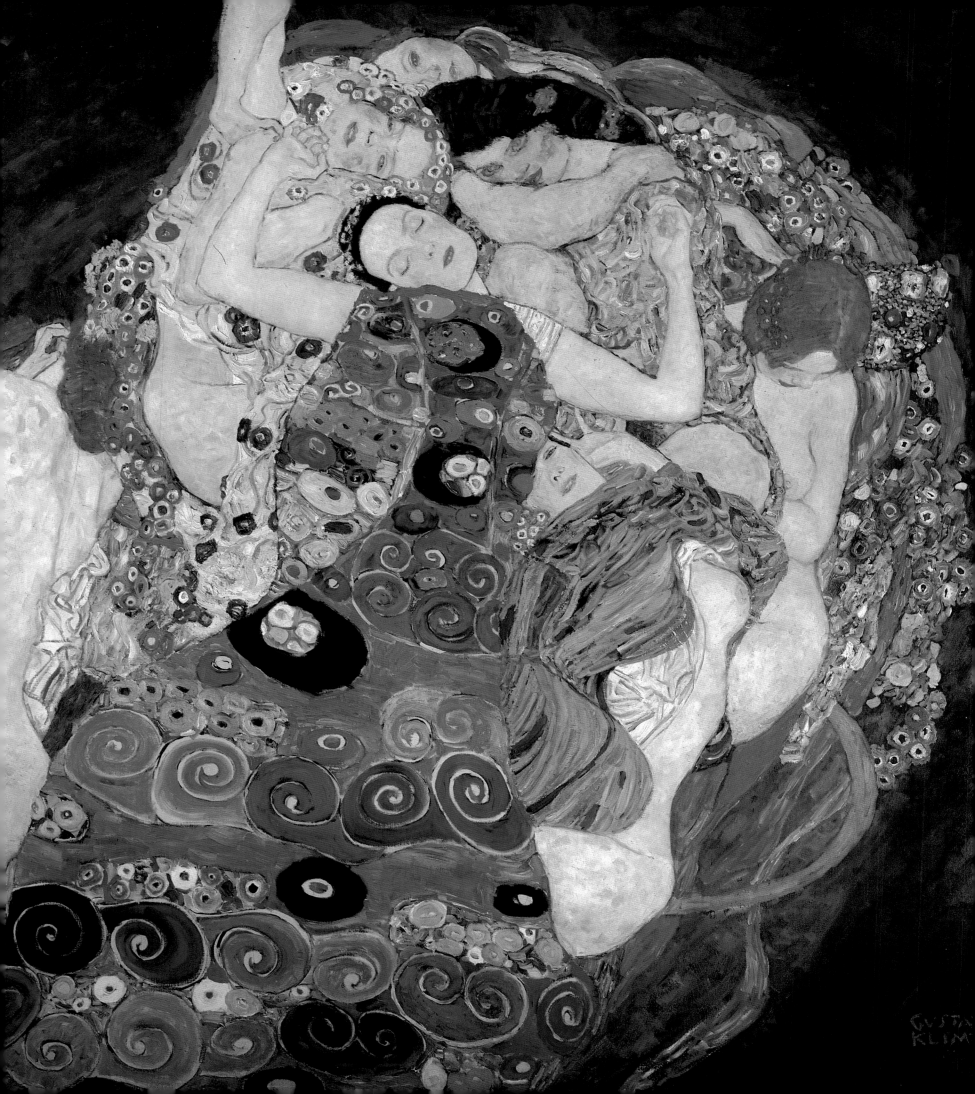

◄49. *Opposite:* Cartoon for the frieze in Stoclet Palace: Expectation, *1905-9; Vienna, Österreichisches Museum für Angewandte Kunst; 193.5 x 115 cm The cartoons were produced for the Wiener Werkstätte mosaic workers for the decoration of the dining room of the Adolphe Stoclet palace, built by the architect Josef Hoffmann for the Belgian magnate Stoclet at Brussels.*
50. *Right:* Cartoon for the frieze in Stoclet Palace: left part of the tree of life, *1905-9; Vienna, Österreichisches Museum für Angewandte Kunst; 197.7 x 105.4 cm*

51. Left: Cartoon for the frieze in
Stoclet Palace: central part of the
tree of life, *1905-9;*
Vienna, Österreichisches Museum für
Angewandte Kunst; 138.8 x 102 cm
Klimt used various techniques for this
work, including tempera,
water color, pastels, pencil,
and gold and silver leaf.
52. Opposite: cartoon for the frieze
in Stoclet Palace:right part of the
tree of life with bushes, *1905-9;* ▶
Vienna, Österreichisches Museum für
Angewandte Kunst; 194.6 x 120.3 cm

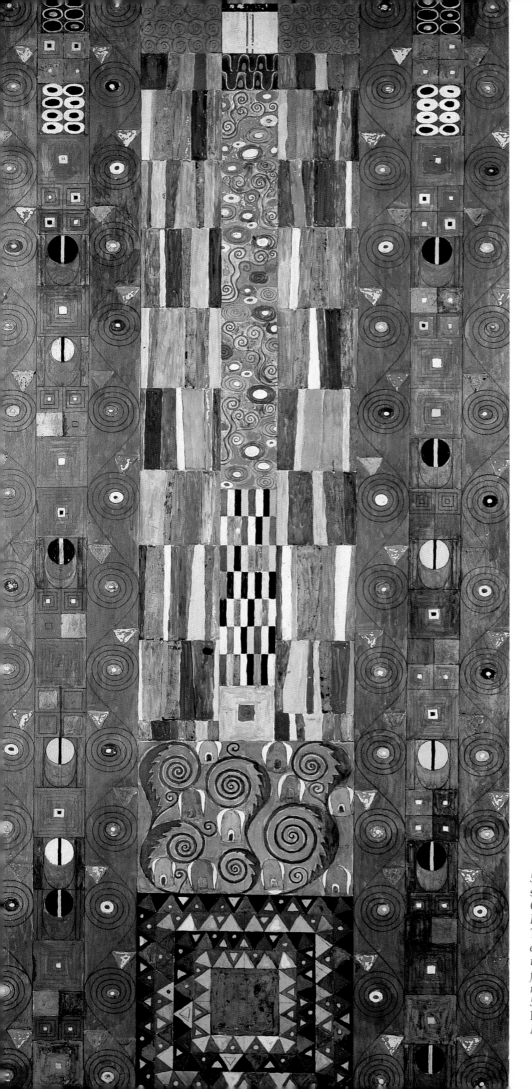

53. Left: Cartoon for the frieze in Stoclet Palace:
separate decorated panel, *1905-9; Vienna,*
Österreichisches Museum für Angewandte
Kunst; 197 x 91 cm
The two-dimensional sense and the use of
enamel, colored glass, and semiprecious stones
in the creation of the frieze are probably derived
from Klimt's memory of the Ravenna
mosaics he had seen in 1903.
54. Opposite: Cartoon for the frieze in Stoclet Palace:
Fulfillment, *1905-9; Vienna, Österreichisches*
Museum für Angewandte Kunst; 194.6 x 120.3 cm ▶

55. Portrait of Johanna Staude, *1917-18; Vienna, Österreichische Galerie; 70 x 50 cm*

56. Portrait of Adele Bloch-Bauer, ca. 1912; Vienna, Österreichische Galerie; 190 x 120 cm
Decorative elements of Japanese origin appear for the first time in this work.

57. Park, *1909-10; New York, Museum of Modern Art (Gertrude A. Mellon Fund); 110.5 x 110.5 cm*
Vegetation is here depicted in a view very close to that of a telephoto lens and thus
takes on an expressive truth of its own.

58. Schloss Kammer on the Attersee, *1910; Vienna, Österreichische Galerie; 110 x 110 cm*
Architectural elements are frequently found in the landscapes of this period. The castle,
in particular, inspired several works.

59. Unterach on the Attersee, 1915; Salzburg, Residenzgalerie; 110 x 110 cm

60. Farmhouse in Upper Austria, *1911-12; Vienna, Österreichische Galerie; 110 x 110 cm*

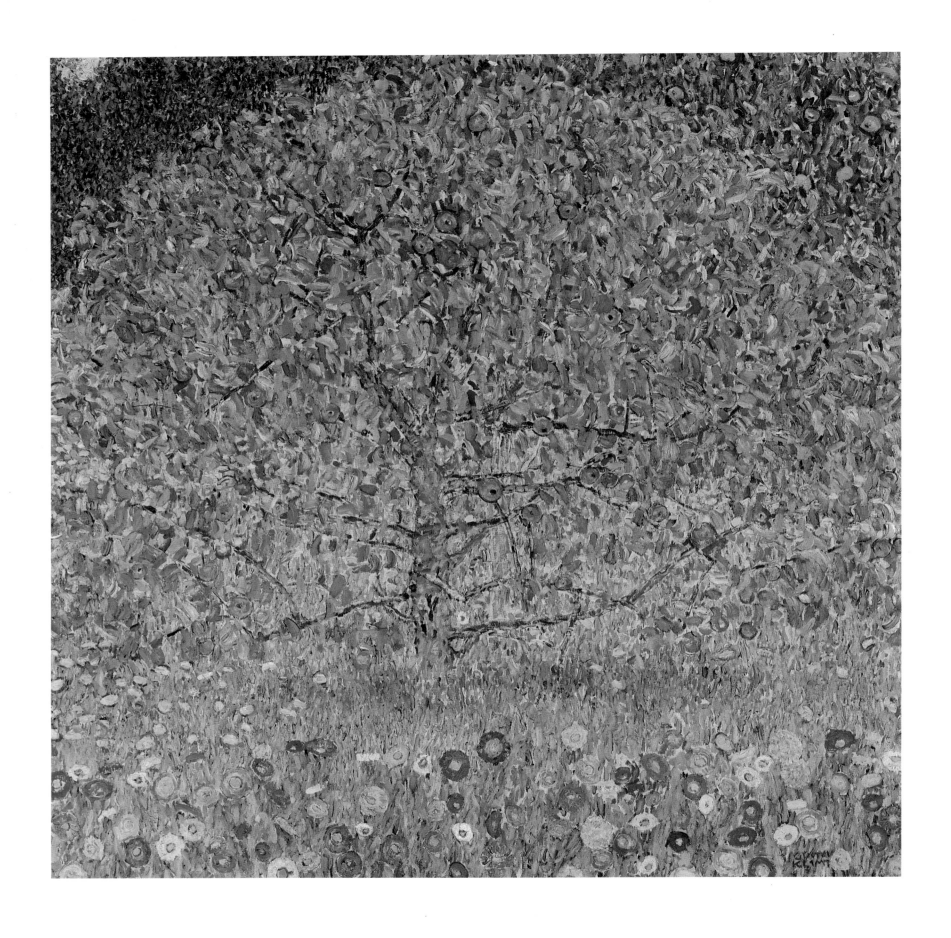

61. Apple Tree, I, ca. 1912; Vienna, Museum des 20, Jahrhunderts (on loan to the Österreichische Galerie); 110 x 110 cm

62. Avenue in Schloss Kammer Park, *1912; Vienna, Österreichische Galerie; 110 x 110 cm*
Klimt's pictorial technique here shows influence of the works of van Gogh.

63. Apple Tree, II, *1916 (?); Vienna, Österreichische Galerie; 80 x 80 cm*

64. Houses at Unterach on the Attersee, ca. 1916; Vienna, Österreichische Galerie; 110 x 110 cm
Klimt here presents a composition in which architecture and nature assume forms of
an almost geometric simplicity.

◄ *65. Opposite:* Portrait of a Lady, *ca. 1916-17; Piacenza,*
Galleria Ricci-Oddi; 60 x 55 cm
66. Right: Portrait of a Lady, *1917-18;*
Linz, Neue Galerie der Stadt Linz, Wolfgang-Gurlitt-
Museum; 180 x 90 cm
This work is unfinished; the body is sketched in,
and the face stands out with its realism
against the incomplete background.

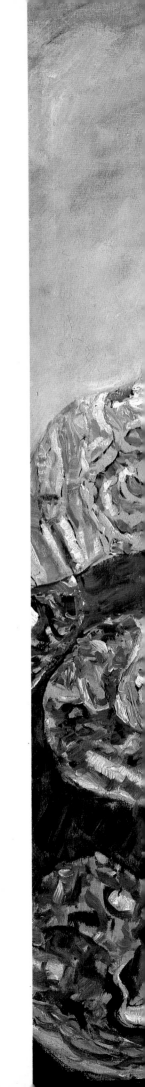

67. Baby (Cradle), *1917-18;*
Washington, D.C., National Gallery of Art; 110 x 110 cm

68. Full-face Portrait of a Lady, *1917-18;*
Linz, Neue Galerie der Stadt Linz, Wolfgang-Gurlitt-Museum; 67 x 56 cm
This work is unfinished.

69. Portrait of a Lady in White, *1917-18; Vienna, Österreichische Galerie; 70 x 70 cm*
Also an unfinished work.

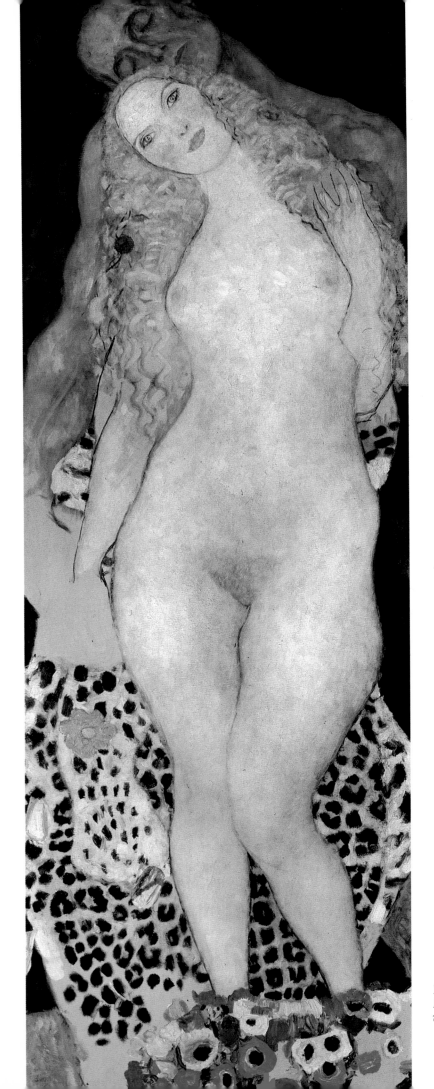

70. Adam and Eve, *1917-18; Vienna, Österreichische Galerie; 173 x 60 cm*
Eve's reclining head and enigmatic smile are reminiscent of other
works by Klimt, such as The Three Ages of Woman *and* The Virgin.

LIST OF PLATES

1. Allegory of Sculpture, *1889*
2. Sculpture, *1896*
3. Tragödie (Tragedy), *1897*
4. Young Girl with Lowered Head, *1898*
5. Junius, *1896*
6. Portrait of a Girl, *1902*
7. Crouching Female Figure, *1908-9*
8. Fable, *1883*
9. Theater in Taormina, *1886-88*
10. Music, I, *1895*
11. Idylle (Idylls), *1884*
12. Auditorium of the Altes Burgtheater, Vienna, *1888*
13. Sappho, *1888-90*
14. Portrait of Joseph Pembauer, *1890*
15. Portrait of a Lady, *1894*
16. Portrait of Sonja Knips, *1898*
17. Portrait of Josef Lewinsky, *1895*
18. Love, *1895*
19. Lady by the Fireplace, *1897-98*
20. Full-face Portrait of a Lady, *1898-99*
21. Pallas Athene, *1898*
22. Portrait of Serena Lederer, *1899*
23. Judith, I, *1901*
24. Portrait of Emilie Flöge, *1902*
25. Cows in a Stall, *1900-1*
26. After the Rain (Garden with Chickens in St. Agatha), *1899*
27. Farmhouse with Birch Trees, *1900*
28. Beech Forest, I, *ca. 1902*
29. The Beethoven Frieze: The Hostile Powers, *1902*
30. The Beethoven Frieze: The Longing for Happiness, *1902*
31. The Beethoven Frieze: The Longing for Happiness Finds Repose in Poetry, *1902*
32. The Beethoven Frieze: The Longing for Happiness Finds Repose in Poetry, *1902.*
33. The Beethoven Frieze: The Longing for Happiness Finds Repose in Poetry, *1902*
34. Hope, I, *1903*
35. Pear Tree, *1903*
36. Farmhouse with Birch Trees, *1903*
37. Farm Garden with Sunflowers, *ca. 1905-6*
38. Portrait of Hermine Gallia, *1904*
39. Portrait of Margaret Stonborough-Wittgenstein, *1905*
40. Portrait of Adele Bloch-Bauer, *1907*
41. Portrait of Fritza Riedler, *1906*
42. Water Serpents, *1904-7*
43. The Three Ages of Woman, *1905*
44. Poppy Field, *1907*
45. Flowering Field, *ca. 1909*
46. The Kiss, *1907-8*
47. Judith, II, *1909*
48. The Virgin, *1912-13*
49. Cartoon for the frieze in Stoclet Palace: Expectation, *1905-9*
50. Cartoon for the frieze in Stoclet Palace: left part of the tree of life, *1905-9*
51. Cartoon for the frieze in Stoclet Palace: central part of the tree of life, *1905-9*
52. Cartoon for the frieze in Stoclet Palace: right part of the tree of life with bushes, *1905-9*
53. Cartoon for the frieze in Stoclet Palace: separate decorated panel, *1905-9*
54. Cartoon for the frieze in Stoclet Palace: Fulfillment, *1905-9*
55. Portrait of Johanna Staude, *1917-18*
56. Portrait of Adele Bloch-Bauer, *ca. 1912*
57. Park, *1909-10*
58. Schloss Kammer on the Attersee, *1910*
59. Unterach on the Attersee, *1915*
60. Farmhouse in Upper Austria, *1911-12*
61. Apple Tree, I, *ca. 1912*
62. Avenue in Schloss Kammer Park, *1912*
63. Apple Tree, II, *1916 (?)*
64. Houses at Unterach on the Attersee, *ca. 1916*
65. Portrait of a Lady, *ca. 1916-17*
66. Portrait of a Lady, *1917-18*
67. Baby (Cradle), *1917-18*
68. Full-face Portrait of a Lady, *1917-18*
69. Portrait of a Lady in White, *1917-18*
70. Adam and Eve, *1917-18*

CHRONOLOGY

1862: On July 14 Gustav Klimt is born at Baumgarten (then a suburb of Vienna); he was the second of seven sons of the family of Ernst Klimt, a goldsmith and engraver from Bohemia, and Anna Finstern, a Viennese woman of modest means.

1876: Klimt begins his studies at the Arts and Crafts Academy of the Austrian Museum for Art and Industry (today Österreichisches Museum für Angewandte Kunst); he attends the two-year preparatory school and then professor Laufberger's school of painting (he stays with Laufberger until the professor's death in 1881).

1879: Together with his brother Ernst and fellow student Franz Matsch, Klimt works with Laufberger's graffiti in the inner courtyard of the Kunsthistorisches Museum in Vienna.

1880: Calling themselves the *Künstlerkompanie*, the group obtains its first commissions: canvases for the salon ceiling of the Sturany Palace in Vienna and the ceiling of the Carlsbad Baths (then Karlovy Vary, in Czechoslovakia).

1881: After the death of Laufberger, Klimt continues to study painting with Viktor Berger; he prepares the publication of his *Allegorien und Embleme* album.

1882: Still with his brother Ernst and Franz Matsch, Klimt works at the Reichenberg Theater, following the style of Hans Makart.

1883: The three open a studio in Vienna, at 8 Sandwirthgasse, and take a trip to Transylvania to the royal castle of Pelesch. Klimt paints *Fable* for *Allegorien und Embleme*.

1884: Klimt studies the Italian Quattrocento, Michelangelo, and Max Klinger; he paints *Idylls*.

1885: The Klimt-Matsch studio, using designs by Makart, works on the decoration of Hermesvilla at Lainz (near Vienna) and of the Community Theater of Fiume.

1886: Klimt begins the work of decorating the two grand staircases of the Burgtheater of Vienna (ceiling and lunette). The work lasts two years.

1888: In recognition of his artistic activity, Klimt receives the Golden Cross from Emperor Franz Josef; he paints, with extraordinary realism, the *Auditorium of the Altes Burgtheater, Vienna.*

1889: Klimt travels to Venice, Trieste, Munich, and Cracow.

1890: Klimt begins the decoration of the intercolumns and lunettes of the grand staircase in the Kunsthistorisches Museum of Vienna.

1891: Klimt joins the association of Viennese artists. They continue the work on the Kunsthistorisches Museum.

1892: After twelve years of working together, the Klimt group moves to a new studio at 21 Josefstädterstrasse (still in Vienna). The deaths of his father (in August) and of his brother Ernst (in December) slow Klimt's artistic activity for some time; nevertheless, his prestige continues to increase. The Munich Secession is founded.

1893: While Franz Matsch prepares a study for the layout of the ceiling and the spandrels of the grand hall of the University of Vienna, Klimt is a guest of Prince Esterhàzy of Totis (Tata), Hungary, where he paints *The Interior of the Esterhàzy Theater of Totis.*

1894: The Matsch-Klimt project for the grand hall of the university is approved. The minister of education commissions the two artists (in actuality, they were growing farther apart) to make sketches of the separate paintings; total compensation for the work is 60,000 florins. An exhibition of Egyptian art and the third exhibition of the Association of Viennese Artists (the prize went to Fernand Khnopff) take place in Vienna.

1895: Klimt paints *Music* and *Love*, with definite symbolistic orientation.

1896: The decorative scheme for the university's grand hall is finally completed: Klimt undertakes the work of the panels representing *Philosophy, Medicine,* and *Jurisprudence* (with the ten pertinent spandrels). During this year (in the *Junius* design) he uses a square format for the first time. The architect Adolf Loos, returned from a trip to America, condemns Klimt's panels: "The ornamentation is a crime."

1897: The Union of Figurative Artists of Austria, the Viennese Secession, is founded; Klimt will shortly become its dominant personality. *Ver Sacrum*, the ideological journal of the movement, is begun.

1898: Klimt participates in the first exhibition of the Secession and, among other things, creates the official manifesto and catalog; he begins intense collaboration as illustrator for *Ver Sacrum*; he paints the portrait of *Sonja Knips.*

1899: Klimt receives notable public success at the fourth exhibition of the Secession with the painting *Schubert at the Piano*; he paints the portrait of *Serena Lederer, Nuda Veritas,* the portrait of *Trude Steiner,* and *Nixies (Silver Fish).*

1900: The sixth exhibition of the Secession is dedicated to Japanese art; in the seventh exhibition, attended by more than 30,000 visitors, Klimt exhibits his first landscape and the incomplete *Philosophy.* The painting arouses intense controversy in Vienna, but at the Universal Exhibition of Paris (in which the Secession participates with 42 works) it wins the gold medal as best foreign work.

1901: *Medicine,* presented at the tenth exhibition of the Secession, sets off harsh reviews and disapproval by the Viennese press; the state legal advisory office asks for seizure of the edition of *Ver Sacrum* containing the preparatory designs for the grand panel, and a group of deputies presents a summons to the minister of education, Von Hartel. Klimt declares himself indifferent to the controversy surrounding his work.

1902: For the fourteenth exhibition of the Viennese Secession, prepared by the architect Josef Hoffmann and entirely dedicated to Beethoven, Klimt creates a seven-part frieze as part of the great *Monument to Beethoven* on three walls of one room of the exhibition; the work arouses controversy, but is admired by Auguste Rodin.

1903: Klimt travels to Ravenna, Venice, and Florence. He continues his decorative works for the University of Vienna (he exhibits them unfinished at the eighteenth showing of the Secession); he reacts to the proposal advanced by the artistic commission of the ministry of education to hang the panels in the Österreichische Galerie. Wiener Werkstätte (United Studios for the Revival and Reorganization of Artisans), which Klimt supports, is created. *Ver Sacrum* concludes its publications.

1904: Klimt participates in exhibitions in Dresden and Munich. He paints *Water Serpents*, his last work exhibited by the Secession. He begins preparing cartoons for the mosaics in the Stoclet Palace dining room, commissioned to Josef Hoffmann by the Belgian magnate Stoclet at Brussels.

1905: Klimt renounces his assignment for the great hall of the university and requests the return of his designs. In May, he buys back the *Jurisprudence, Medicine,* and *Philosophy* panels from the ministry of education; he paints the portrait of *Margaret Stonborough-Wittgenstein* and *The Three Ages of Woman.*

1906: Internal dissent within the Secession leads to an open break: the secessionists led by Klimt form a new group called Kunstschau, or, more commonly, "Klimt group" (Otto Wagner and Josef Hoffmann were part of the group). Klimt paints *Fritza Riedler,* the first of the great portraits of his golden period.

1907: The last modifications to the sketches for the university are made; Klimt paints *The Kiss,* the first portrait of *Adele Bloch-Bauer,* and *Poppy Field;* he meets Egon Schiele, then seventeen years old, for the first time.

1908: In the summer Klimt inaugurates the "Kunstschau Wien 1908," first official show by the Klimt group (Oskar Kokoschka also participates and makes the poster); Klimt delivers the inaugural address and exhibits sixteen works. He paints *Life and Death* and travels to Florence.

1909: Klimt presides over the second Kunstschau, dedicated to contemporary foreign art (including van Gogh, Munch, Gauguin, Bonnard, Vuillard, and Matisse), and exhibits *Judith II* and *Old Lady.* He participates in the tenth International Exposition in Munich and in the eighteenth exhibition of the Berlin Secession; he travels to Prague, Paris, and Spain. At Wiener Werkstätte, the preparatory work for the Stoclet Palace mosaics is begun under his direction.

1910: Klimt participates in the ninth Biennial International Exhibition of Modern Art in Venice (among his paintings are *Mothers and Sons* and *The Black Feather Hat*) and achieves notable success; he is also present at the exhibition of the Deutsche Künstlerbund (the league of German artists) in Prague.

1911: Klimt spends time in Florence and Rome, where he receives *ex aequo* the first prize at the International Exposition of Art; in the course of the year he travels to Brussels, London, and Madrid. The great mosaic frieze, wherein Klimt's symbolization process through decorative elements achieves maturity, is mounted at Stoclet Palace.

1912: A period of intense pictorial activity commences; the portraits of this year (*Adele Bloch-Bauer, II,* among them) signal the beginning of the so-called ornate style. Klimt participates in the Grand Art Exhibition of Dresden; for the first time he goes to Bad Gastein for thermal cures.

1913: Klimt participates in the exhibitions of the League of Austrian Artists in Budapest and in the third exhibition of the League of German Artists at the Kunsthalle of Mannheim; he completes *The Virgin,* which was later exhibited at the eleventh International Exposition of Art

in Munich. He passes the summer at Malcesine, on Lake Garda.

1914: Klimt once again attends the exhibit of the League of German Artists, which takes place in Prague; he goes on a trip to Brussels and Rome. War breaks out during the summer. In Germany, under the influence of the expressionistic theory, criticism of Klimt begins.

1915: He paints the portraits of *Barbara Flöge* and *Charlotte Pulitzer;* he lives and works in Györ, Hungary.

1916: Klimt participates (together with Schiele, Kokoschka, and Faistauer) in the exhibition of Austrian artists at the Berlin Secession; he paints the portrait of *Friederike Maria Beer* and some landscapes, among then *Schönbrunn Park.*

1917: Klimt travels in northern Moravia, to Tyrol (during the summer), and again in Rumania; he paints *Baby, Leda, Friends,* and *Lady with a Fan;* he is nominated as an honorary member to the Academy of Fine Arts in Vienna and the Academy of Munich.

1918: Upon returning from his trip in Rumania, Klimt suffers a stroke on January 11; on February 6 he dies in a Vienna hospital. Egon Schiele creates an intense portrait of Klimt on his deathbed. A large number of incomplete works remains in his studio. Schiele, Hodler, Koloman Moser, and Otto Wagner die during the same year.

MUSEUMS AND COLLECTIONS

The following is a geographical guide to the principal museums and private collections that have works by Klimt. The number of works in each holding is indicated.

About twenty paintings and many drawings by Klimt were destroyed in a fire in Immendorf castle (May 1945) started by Soviet occupation troops.

Basel (Switzerland). Kunstmuseum: 2
Beverly Hills (California). Gruen Collection: 1
Cambridge (Massachusetts). Busch-Reisinger Museum, Harvard University: 1
  Fogg Art Museum, Harvard University: 1
Carlsbad (Czechoslovakia). Baths Salon: 1
  Municipal Theater:. 3
Dallas (Texas). Private collection: 1
Dresden (Germany). Staatliche Kunstsammlungen, Gemäldegalerie Neue Meister: 1
Ferlach (Carinthia). Schwab-Trau Collection: 2
Geneva (Switzerland). Erich Lederer Collection: 2
Graz (Austria). Victor Fogarassy Collection: 2
  Private collection: 5
Holland. Private collection: 1
Honolulu (Hawaii). Private collection: 4
Innsbruck (Austria). Tiroler Landesmuseum Ferdinandeum: 1
Kansas City (Missouri). Bruce Goff Collection: 1
Lainz (Vienna). Hermesvilla: 1
London (Great Britain). National Gallery: 1
Lugano (Switzerland). Ephraim Collection: 1
Munich (Germany). Bayerische Staatgemäldesammlungen, Neue Pinakothek: 2

Private collection: 1
New York (New York). Beer-Monti Collection: 1
  Hanna Spitzer Collection: 1
  Collection of Dr. and Mrs. Otto Kallir: 1
  Museum of Modern Art: 1
  St. Etienne Gallery: 1
  Selected Artists Galleries: 1
  Private collection: 1
Norman (Oklahoma). University of Oklahoma Museum of
  Art: 1
Ottawa (Canada). National Gallery of Canada: 1
Paris (France). Felix Landau Collection: 1
  Private collection: 1
Pelesch (Sinaia). Castello Reale: 1
Piacenza (Italy). Galleria Ricci-Oddi: 1
Pittsburgh (Pennsylvania). Museum of Art, Carnegie
  Institute: 1
Prague (Czechoslovakia). Národní Galerie: 3
Rijeka (Yugoslavia). Municipal Theater: 1
Rome (Italy). Galleria Nazionale d'Arte Moderna: 1
Salzburg (Austria). Residenzgalerie: 1
Scarsdale (New York). Winter Collection: 1
Solothurn (Switzerland). Private collection: 1
Venice (Italy). Galleria d'Arte Moderna: 1
Vienna (Austria). Albertina: 5
  Burgtheater: 3
  Marko Danilovatz Collection: 3
  Helene Donner Collection: 3
  Richard Parzer Collection: 1
  Marietta Preleuthner Collection: 1
  Tan-Bunzl Collection: 1
  Galerie Wurthle: 1
  Österreichische Galerie: 24
  Österreichische Nationalbibliotek, Theatersammlung
  (Hermann Bahr/Anna Bahr– Mildenburg– Gedenk-
  raum): 1
  Historisches Museum der Stadt Wien: 9
  Kunsthistorisches Museum: 3
  Museum des 20. Jahrhunderts: 1
  Österreichisches Museum für Angewandte Kunst: 3
  Sturany Palace: 3
  Zentralsparkasse der Gemeinde Wien: 1
  Zierer Palace: 1
  Private collections: 23
Winnipeg (Canada). Ferdinand Eckhardt Collection: 1
Zurich (Switzerland). Collection of the Federal College of
  Technology: 1

Location unknown: 48
Works lost: 5
Works destroyed: 20

ESSENTIAL BIBLIOGRAPHY

Art in Vienna, from the Secession to the Fall of the Hapsburg Empire, exhibition catalog of the Venice biennial, 1984
Bahr, H. *Gegen Klimt,* Vienna-Leipzig, 1903
—. *Rede uber Klimt,* Vienna, 1901
Bahr, H., and Altenberg, P. *Das Werk Gustav Klimts,* Vienna, 1918
Bouillon, J.P. *Klimt: Beethoven,* Geneva, 1986
Breicha, O., editor. *Gustav Klimt,* Milan, 1981
Comini, A. *Gustav Klimt,* New York, 1975
Coradeschi, S., editor. *Klimt,* in "Classici dell'Arte," Rizzoli, Milan, 1982
Dobai, J. *Introduction to catalog of exhibition of Klimt and Egon Schiele at the Guggenheim Museum,* New York, 1965
Dobai, J., and Coradeschi, S. *L'opera completa di Klimt,* Milan, 1978
Eisler, M. *Gustav Klimt,* Vienna, 1920
Gustav Klimt – Disegni erotici, Mazzotta, Milan, 1980
Hatle, I. *Gustav Klimt, Ein Wiener Maler des Jugendstils,* Vienna, 1958
Hevesi, L. *Acht Jahre Sezession, 1897-1905,* Vienna, 1906
—. *Altkunst-Neukunst, Wien 1894-1908,* Vienna, 1918
Hofmann, W. *Gustav Klimt,* Salzburg, 1971
—. *Moderne Malerei in Osterreich,* Vienna, 1965
Liechtenstein, M.J. *Gustav Klimt und seine oberösterreichischen Salzkammergutlandschaften,* in "Oberösterreichische Heimatblätter," nos. 3-4, 1951
—. *Kunst in Österreich, 1815-1951,* Linz, 1951
Moll, C. *Ricordo Gustav Klimt,* Vienna, 1943
Nakayama, K. *Klimt,* Tokyo, 1985
Nebehay, C.M. *Gustav Klimt. Sein Leben nach zeitgenösischen Berichten und Quellen,* Munich, 1976
—. *Gustav Klimt Dokumentation,* Vienna, 1969
—. *Gustav Klimt – 150 Bedeutende Zeichnungen,* Vienna, 1962
—. *Gustav Klimt, Eine Nachlese, 70 Bedeutende Zeichnungen,* Graz, 1964
—. *Ver Sacrum, 1898-1903,* Dortmund, 1987
Novotny, F., and Dobai, J. *Gustav Klimt,* Salzburg, 1967 (this work presents the most extensive bibliography currently available on Klimt, together with a large quantity of information on the artist's life and work)
Pirchan, E. *Gustav Klimt,* Vienna, 1956 (includes a catalog of paintings compiled by A. Grunberg)
—. *Gustav Klimt, Ein Kunstler aus Wien,* Vienna, 1942
Powell, N. *The Sacred Spring: The Arts in Vienna, 1898-1918,* London, 1974
Sabarsky, S., editor. *Gustav Klimt,* exhibition catalog of the Isetan Museum of Art, Tokyo, 1981
—. editor. *Gustav Klimt,* exhibition catalog of the Musées Royaux des Beaux-Arts de Belgique, Brussels, 1987
—. editor. *Gustav Klimt, 100 disegni,* Mazzotta, Milan, 1984
—. et al. *Gustav Klimt,* Milan, 1986
Schorske, C.E. *Fin-de-Siècle Vienna, Politics and Culture,* New York, 1961
Strobl, A. *Gustav Klimt,* Salzburg, 1962-1965
—. *Gustav Klimt–Die Zeichnungen,* Salzburg, 1980
—. *Gustav Klimt, 1862-1918, Zeichnungen,* exhibition catalog of Graphische Sammlung, Albertina, Vienna, 1962
—. *Gustav Klimt, 25 Zeichnungen,* Graz, 1964
Vergo, P. *Art in Wien, 1898-1918,* London, 1975
Vienne, 1880-1938, l'apocalypse joyeuse, catalog of the Georges Pompidou Center, Paris, 1986

For the color illustrations, thanks are due the museums and private and public collections cited in the captions as well as Artothek (Planneg), Fotostudio Otto (Vienna), Georg Mayer (Vienna), Giorgio Vasari (Rome), Reale Fotografia Giacomelli (Venice), and Studio Fotografico F.lli Manzotti (Piacenza). For the black-and-white illustrations: Museum der Stadt Wien (Vienna).

Printed in January 1991
by Amilcare Pizzi S.p.A., Cinisello Balsamo (Milan) Italy